HOW ROBOTS CAN BRING POSITIVE EMOTION

TO TRAVELLERS

JOHN LOK

ISBN 979-888569858-0

Contents

Preface

This book aims to explain why and how future artificial intelligent technology (big data gathering method) can be applied to assit businesses to predict why and when and how consumer behavior changes. I shall explain why traditional psychological and statistic and marketing methods are applied to predict consumer behaviors, human's judgement and analytical effort will be worse to compare AI machine's judgement and analytical effort.

Also, I shall indicate different business organizations why they apply AI big data gathering method to help them to design any questionnaires (surveys) questions which will be more valid and useful to conclude human's questionnaires (surveys) design questions method. Can AI build positive consumption or leisure emotion to consumers in order to avoid negative emotion to consumers? I shall attempt to apply psychological and machine method to explain this question. Readers can have more clear understanding whether AI can be good tool to build positive consumer emotion.

Prologue

Table of contents

What is actively based patterns of urban population of travel behavioral prediction method?
What is trip based versus activity based approaches?
Can apply (AI) big data gathering method predict senior age will be main travelling target?
IS (AI) big data gathering method a better psychological method to compare human marketing research method predict travel behavioral consumption?
How can apply (AI) digital channel
(big data gathering method) predict
travelling consumer behaviors?
Reference p.226-229

Chapter 7

What factors can influence travel behavioural consumption

Prediction travel behavioral consumption from psychology view and computer statistic view. p.230-240

Whether climate change can influence travelling behaviours.

Market method predicts future
travel consumption behavior p.241-243

Whether individual habitual behaviour can influence travelling behaviour: e.g. renting
travel transportation tools

How to determine future travel behavior from past travel experience and perceptions of risk and safety for the benefits to travel consumers?

What is push and pull factors to influence any
traveler who chooses where is whose preferable travelling destination.

Why expectation, motivation and attitude factor can influence travelling behaviour.

What methods can predict future travel behavioural consumption p.244-254

How to use qualitative of travel behavioural method to predict future travel consumption.

How to apply advanced traveler information systems (ATIS) to predict future travelling behaviour.

How does online tourism sale channel can influence traveling consumption of behaviour.

Actively based patterns of urban population of travel behavioural prediction method.

What is trip based versus activity based approaches?

Why senior age will be main travelling target.

Psychological method to predict
travel behavioural consumption.

Reference p.255

Chapter 8

Main barriers influence artificial intelligence
consumer behavioral prediction

(AI) digital data gather technology predicts food consumer behavior's main barriers
p.256-276

The challenges of (AI) big data gather shaping
the future of retail for consumer industries

Challenge to using (AI) neural networks to predict customer behavior from big data
gather tool

Challenges of artificial intelligence, algorithms technology and machine learning impact to consumption market

Is Artificial Intelligent the most effective and
accurate consumer behavioral tool?

Bibliography

CHAPTER ONE

AI prediction consumer behavior tool

Nowadays, many businessmen or marketing research professional hope to apply different methods to predict consumer behaviors in order to know what will be future market activities and market changes to help them to choose to implement what kinds of marketing strategies more accurately. The methods include economic environmental change prediction method, consumer individual psychological change prediction method, micro or macro behavioral economic environmental change prediction method, marketing environmental change prediction method etc. different kinds of methods which can be applied to predict how consumer behavioral changes to influence whose behavioral consumption to the manufacturer products sale within one to two years short term or three to five years middle term, even above five years long term business plans.Hence, if the product manufacturers can apply the most suitable consumer behavioral prediction method to predict how consumers‘ choice will be changed to influence their products sale easily. It will have more beneficial intangible and tangible advantages to achieve the their product easier sale aim to ensure their businesses' future market share to be increased more easier to their countries‘ choice target sale markets. Otherwise, if they applied the inaccurate consumer behavioral prediction methods to predict how their consumers' behavioral changes wrongly. Then, it will influence their market shares to be same level, even it will decrease their market shares, when their consumer behavioral prediction inaccurately.

In my this book first part, I concentrate on indicate whether any artificial intelligence (AI) tools will be one kind of good consumer behavioral prediction method to be choose to apply to predict consumer behaviors. I shall indicate some examples, cases to give reasonable evidences to analyze whether (AI) tools will be one kind suitable tool to be applied to predict when and how consumer behavioral changes. If (AI) can be one kind tool to attempt to be applied to predict when and how consumer behavioral changes. Will it replace other kinds of methods to predict consumer behaviors? Does it have weaknesses to be applied to predict consumer behaviors, instead of strengths? Can it be applied to predict consumer behaviors depending on any situations of only some situation? Finally, I believe that any readers can find answers to answer above these questions in this book.

In my this book second part, I shall explain why and how human can possible apply (AI) tool to predict consumer individual emotion. I shall indicate case studies to explain how consumer individual better or worse emotion how to influence whose consumption behavior in different situation. Finally, I shall indicate evidences to conclude how and why (AI) tool that can be used to predict consumer individual emotion and it will have direct relationship to influence consumption behavior, as well as how (AI) tool can assist businessmen to judge whether what reasons case the customer does not choose to buy its product, it is possible because the product high price factor, poor product quality or poor staff service performance or attitude etc. different factors to influence the consumer decides to choose to buy the other product consequently, when the (AI) tool can confirm consumer has good or bad emotion to judge what factors are the causes his decision making at the moment.

Readers can understand why and how (AI) tool can be attempt to be applied to predict customer emotion and it can influence positive or negative consumption behavior to the product clearly in this part.

In my this book, I concentrate on indicate whether any artificial intelligence (AI) tools will be one kind of good consumer behavioral prediction method to be choose to apply to predict consumer behaviors. I shall indicate some examples, cases to give reasonable evidences to analyze whether (AI) tools will be one kind suitable tool to be applied to predict when and how consumer behavioral changes. If (AI) can be one kind tool to attempt to be applied to predict when and how consumer behavioral changes. Will it replace other kinds of methods to predict consumer behaviors? Does it have weaknesses to be applied to predict consumer behaviors, instead of strengths? Can it be applied to predict consumer behaviors depending on any situations of only some situation? Finally, I believe that any readers can find answers to answer above these questions in this book. However, artificial intelligence and machine learning can help any vehicle manufacturers to find solution to solve patterns in highly to solve patterns in highly complex data-sets that are beyond the capability of a human brain, and then building and automatically acting on the customer insights it generates.

Given the automotive customer need for individualized communications, this technology is positioned to become a critical component of any successful vehicle retailer's domestic or/and overseas vehicle markets. How can vehicle manufacturers and retailers use (AI) to enhance their vehicle marketing campaigns? How will (AI) affect their vehicle sale marketing strategy? What criteria would they use when selecting on (AI) solution?

Vehicle consumers today are able to quickly access different brands of vehicle information, research vehicle products and reviews, negotiate prices and compare one vehicle brand or retailer to another resulting of the brands of vehicle customers. At the same time, the rise of " big -data mining", wearable devices that track user's every move and preference and greater contextualization in advertising and social media has resulted in consumer expectations of individualized. Thus, it seems that (AI) tools can be used to gather " big-data" and then they can make human's mind to analyze how to design kinds of vehicles to satisfy vehicle buyers' needs.

As automotive vehicle marketers can apply (AI) tools to achieve messaging strategies to meet the needs of this new generation of informed vehicle consumers, using data from a variety of sources to move from a variety of sources to move from mass- messaging to more personalized messages aimed at particular vehicle buyer segments, e.g. fast speed sport vehicle buyer segment, slow speed comfortable small size or large size of buyer segment. However, when 90% of vehicle marketers believe having a single vehicle buyer view is important, only 6% have achieved it.

However, one of the main issues vehicle marketers facing is the lack of capacity to efficiently sift through and analyze the massive vehicle buyer amounts of data required to create vehicle buyer individualized vehicle customer experiences easily. This is especially difficult for automotive dealers, the long periods between purchase cycles, and the highly considered nature of the vehicle purchase means that each vehicle dealer needs to not only track a large number of potential vehicle customers for an extremely long period of time, but each of those vehicle customers will generate a huge amount of different kinds of vehicle behavioral consumption data as they research their next vehicle purchase. However, by choosing the right (AI) technological tools and programs , vehicle dealers can solve this big data gathering challenge into a major advantage.

For Forrester vehicle brand example, vehicle consumers have more power over the Forrester vehicle brand's reputation than ever before. Mayne, L. (2014) indicated that Forrester calls this new (AI) tools is the " age of the vehicle customer", a 20 year business cycle in which the most successful vehicle enterprises will reinvent themselves to systematically understand and serve increasingly powerful vehicle consumers. To win in this new age, Forrester declares companies must become vehicle customer obsessed and the only sustainable competitive advantage is knowledge and engagement with customers, such as (AI) gathering data knowledge.

Thus, the biggest challenge vehicle businesses currently face is not the collection of a large quantity of vehicle consumer data, but what to do with that data once they have it. Even at a large vehicle data research firm, the data sets are often too big for a single analyze, or even a team of analysts to sort through and draw conclusion from. However, enter artificial intelligence and machine learning , an efficient technology solution that can continuously find patterns in highly complex data sets that are way beyond the capacity of a human brain and then automatic drive action based on the customer insights is generated.

What is (AI) machine learning tool? Machine learning is a type of (AI) that learns from data and is not explicitly program. Think Amazon, face book. Machine learning serves up relevant content based on an individual vehicle purchase behavior and experiences. More simply, machine learning is a computer program that can learn relationships between data, subject those learnings to errors functions, and then learn from its errors. The program in effect, trains itself.

Lee, T. (2016) explained that "Thus, (AI) tools can learn deep a more advanced branch of machine learning inspired by how our brain's nervous function, has also been found to be especial effective in identifying patterns from data."

When this way sound is complicated from a vehicle dealer perspective, the implementation of a marketing program driven by artificial intelligence can take care of these tasks in an automatic vehicle fashion with little to no manual intervention required from the staff at time vehicle stores.

In practice at a vehicle dealership, the program will continue track vehicle customer behavior online, merging that data with any offline source (like

CRM or DMS data) and then analyze this aggregated vehicle buyer data set to predict what vehicle customer may be shopping for and what information they might like to relevance from different kinds style of vehicle design photos.

1.1 Why can (AI) be applied to predict consumer behaviors?

Artificial intelligence refers to complex in vehicle market, machine learning that posses the same characteristics of human intelligence and that have all our sense, all our reason and think just like human do. Besides, machine learning is the practice of using algorithms to collect and examine data, learn from it, and then make a determination or prediction about something in the world.

The machine is " trained" using large amounts of data and algorithms that give it the ability to learn how to automatically perform a task with increasing accuracy. Otherwise, deep learning is primarily based on artificial neural networks inspired by our understanding of the biology of human's brains.

Deep learning breaks down tasks in ways that enables machines to assist us with increasingly complex tasks, driverless cars, better preventive healthcare and more accurate product recommendation (including vehicle recommendations). So, such as why (AI) technology can be applied to predict how vehicle consumer behavior changes to bring to judge whether vehicle consumer will like what kinds of vehicle styles next year. Then, vehicle manufacturers can gather overall vehicle consumer data to analyze and conclude the more accurate vehicle design direction for next year any new design vehicle manufacturing products.

Thus, (AI) machine learning can help vehicle manufacturers to solve how to design any new vehicle products challenge. A vehicle is both one of the most important and carefully considered purchases the majority of people will ever make in their lifetime. It is also a purchase that tends to be fundamentally tied to a person's identify and view of themselves. As the same time, vehicle consumers changing lifestyles result in changing vehicle needs, e.g. the young sport car enthusiast matures into the family driver.

Automotive dealers need to remember that vehicle customers and prospects are individual human beings with risk, complex and ever-changing lives factors, these factors will influence every vehicle consumer why who feels has vehicle purchase need, and how who choose to buy the first vehicle if who decided to buy the first vehicle.

The (AI) technological customer behavioral prediction tool seems to be the best vehicle salespeople in the world are those that know every one of their vehicle customers. Their likes and dislikes which style of vehicle design, preferences and changing tastes to vehicle choices. The capacity of the human brain, however, limits us from achieving this type of vehicle sales and frequent turnover at vehicle dealerships often results in the further loss of vehicle salespeople along with their vehicle customer relationships and knowledge. In this competitive vehicle environment, machine learning enables platforms to assist the vehicle sales team by tracking the vehicle consumer behaviors of each vehicle customer, learning and memorizing their preferences and predicting their future vehicle purchase needs.

Finally, I recommend that for a vehicle dealerships marketing platform to make their customer engagement efficient and fully-functional, I should be able to: applying (AI) tools to track every vehicle customer behavior across the web, connecting to a society of data sources, CRM, DMS, third-party, web vehicle brands, social email, click etc., aggregating and accurately cross-reference data from a variety of sources, leveraging this data to drive insights on a mass scale, as well as on an individualized basis, driving actions and automatically direct customer engagement via multiple channels based on where each customer is in their individual lifecycle.

1.2 How can (AI) provide businesses with better-informed decisions

I shall explain how (AI) technology can provide businesses with better-informed decisions to drive top-line growth, deliver meaningful experience for customers and smooth their path along the consumer journey. The widely understood definition of (AI) involves the ability of machines or computers to learn human thinking, reasoning and decision-making abilities.

A Narrative science study in 2015 year identified that (AI) was being used primarily in voice recognition, machine learning virtual assistants and decision support. This study also highlighted the many branches of (AI) and that techniques and their definition are used interchangeably. It is possible that (AI) can be used to gather big data , then to analyze to help businesses to predict consumer behaviors. For example, one of the most common techniques is machine learning, where algorithms are used to perform tasks by learning from historical data. Another growth branch of (AI) is natural language procession.

However, during 2017 year, search engines will begin to factor additional behavioral data into prediction of customer behavioral results, such as the user's history of searches and locations and previously captures conservations. Artificial intelligence will use this information to power predictive search results, e.g. predictive future consumer's choice behavioral processing for any kinds of businesses.

Predictive search will improve the quality of search results, and provide new insights into consumers' behavior and the moments which matter to them. Search will give recommendation into tailored how consumer individual choice in consumption process. Several of the largest online platforms already use machine learning to improve predictive consumer behavioral search results.

For example, Google's rank brain technology adds research by understanding the context in which the consumer has entered it. Over time, rank brain will learn further from user behaviors Amazon's DSSTNE (pronouned destiny) learns from shoppers' purchasing habits and consumption behavior to offer better product recommend actions, which Amazon can offer before a consumer has entered anything into the search bar. However, this technology is not independent of human input. For example, Google engineers will periodically retain the rank brain system to improve the models it uses. For another example, in 2016 year , Apple computer revamped its photos app to allow consumers to search for specific items in the phots, they want to find, not just dates and locations. Each photo that an intelligent phone or intelligent pad user takes goes through 11 billion computations, so that photos can understand exactly what is the photography.

It seems that in future, (AI) machine learning will allow search to evolve even further. Search engineers will deliver refined recommendations to their business users and use less human input to predict consumers' needs. For IBM computer example, it indicated 90% of the data that exists today has been created in the last two years. This huge explosion of data gives brands the opportunity to quickly spot and react to the latest trends, fashion and fads among its clients and potential clients. This will allow companies to better engage with younger consumers, who gain influence access to the latest trends, and use the brands. They associate with to help define who they are as individuals. Thus, brands have to identify and make use of them before consumers move on, but the vast quantity of data available makes. This a resource-intensive task. For next example, Lesara, a based online clothes store, uses this machine learning to inform its product decision often gathering information from internal and external sources. When its trends -spotting shoes. Lesara has a range of over 20 styles and sells hundreds of pairs a day. It focus on giving consumers, the very latest trends allow Lesara to develop on average of 50,000 new items each year. It compared to 11,000 old items each year. Thus, (AI) brain seems to human brain to own analytical ability to predict consumer behaviors.

For another example, Lesara is one online clothes store, uses machine learning decisions after gathering information from internal and external sources. One of its most popular products, shoes with LED started life when its trend spotting software flagged up a blogger wearing similar shoes. Now Lesara has a range of over 20 styles and sells hundreds of pairs a day. Its focus on giving consumers the very latest trends allows Lesara to develop an average of 50,000 new items each year, compared to 11,000 for its competitor Lara. it seems (AI) machine learning can help Lesara business to predict what kinds of shoes design or style that shoe consumers will prefer choose to buy in future shoe market trend. Thus, Lesara can predict shoe consumers‘ taste successfully and it can manufacture many attractive style of shoes. (AI) machine learning can gather global past shoe consumer's shoe shopping experiences, then analyzes to make conclusion to give lesara recommendation successfully. This will make the experience more enjoyable for shoe consumers and allow Lesara to advert whose different new style or design of shoes to deliver them move relevant messages by understanding the context of the experience.

However, (AI) machine learning will have this risk who manufacturers need to concern if they applied this technology to predict consumer behavior. It is on sample consumers' privacy issue, in order to avoid complaint chance occurrence. However, machine learning can tie this data together to identify which f the billions of devices are being used by individual consumers. This helps brands understand how consumer engagement and actions can be attributed to different messages in different contexts and at different time. So, machine learning can help brands to build confidence to promote their products by any advertisement channels. When, this new (AI) machine learning technology can conclude how to design their products to be the most attractive, due to it has more accurate to predict consumer behaviors to compare human themselves prediction judgement effort. It seems that (AI) machine judgement effort is more accurate to compare to human judgment effort.

For example, google is moving away from cookies and using logged in data to track and make to users. It plans to expand the scope of the brand lift tool from online video. Thus, consumers are responded will to shippable context, finding it persuasive and easy to navigate by (AI) machine learning decision. For example, fashion brands can aggregate their You tub videos and blogs into a mobile context marketing experience, such as brand centric context into a personal shopping activity gives the shopper an experience, who are likely to remember and tell their friends about any new style of products design promotion from these internet advertisement channels after (AI) machine learning tools‘ styles of product design recommendation.

Chapter Two

What is (AI) deep learning techniques to forecast environment behavioral consumption

The (AI) deep-learning technology leads to performance enhancement and generalization of artificial intelligent technology. It influences the global leader in the field of information technology has declared its intention to utilize the deep-learning technology to solve environmental problems, such as climate change. So, it will help agriculture farming businesses can raise any plant food: vegetable, fruit, rice which grow up very easily if farmers can apply (AI) deep-learning technology to solve environment problems to influence their plant food grow. If the whole year seasonal change is very good and it is suitable for any plant food to grow in farming land easily, e.g. rain is enough and soil is enough for any plant food to grow in the farm lands. Then, fruit, rice, vegetable etc. agriculture businesses will have much beneficial attribution to global farmers.

The question is how to use deep-learning technologies in the environmental field to predict the status of pro-environmental consumption. We predicted the pro-environmental consumption index based on Google search query data, using a recurrent neural network (RNN model). To certify the accuracy of the index, we compared the prediction accuracy of the RNN model with that of the ordinary least square and artificial necessary network models. For example, the RNN model predicts the pro-environmental consumption index better than any other model. we expect the RNN model to perform still better in a big data environment because the deep-learning technologies would be increasingly as the volume of data grows. So, deep-learning technologies could be useful in environmental forecasting to prevent damage caused by climate change to influence any rice, vegetable, tomato, potato, fruit etc. different plant food grow in any countries' farming land easily.

For South Korea example, over 800 government agencies spent 2.2 trillion Korea won on eco-products in 2014 year. However, green products are rarely purchased outside these agencies. This phenomenon occurs because there is a gap between consumer attitudes and behavior , that is environmental attitude is a major factor in decision making vis-a-vis the consumption of " green" food and services (Jorea Ministry of Environment, 2015). Therefore, it is necessary to understand those consumer attitude, that will lead to sustainability-conductive behavior and consumption.

2.1 Environmental consumption prediction

Recently, many researchers have studied pro-environmental consumption and household indexes as well as suicide rate predictions using messages posted by internet users on Google trend, Tweets etc. channel. Whether can environmental consumption be predicted by (AI) deep-learning technological internet channel? How can impact the pro-environmental consumption attitudes of green policies? Korea scientists estimated pro-environmental attitudes using search query data provided by Google trend and confirmed through regression analysis, that pro-environmental attitude has a positive correlation with the pro-environmental attitude index. They also explained that environment-friendly attitude of residents plan an important role in policy making. In the past, most household consumption indexed were calculated through surveys, but (AI) deep-learning technological tool " big data" have recently gained research attention (Lee et al. 2016).

It seems that (AI) deep-learning technology can help agricultural export countries' farmers , e.g. US, UK, Canada, New Zealand, Australia, Japan, China, India etc. they can predict environmental behavioral consumption to any rice, tomato, potato , fruit, vegetable etc. plant food consumers. The beneficial advantages to them include as below:

(a) Assuming they know their countries' weather, when it has less rain to cause drought or when it has more rain in any seasonal time in the year. They can choose not to grow any kinds of above these plant food to avoid loss.

(b) They can make any kinds of above these plant food price raising after their prediction of these bad seasonal time to cause their plant food shortage supply challenge. Because these plant food consumers' demand number is more, but the supply of these above plant food supply number is less. However, due to they had predicted when the bad seasonal time can not allow them to grow these above plant food before. So, they have enough time to grow many these above plant food number in predictive good seasonal time to prepare to supply to their plant food import countries' plant food consumers to eat. Thus, these predictive environmental consumption plant food export countries can raise their plant food price to sell to them. When, the other non-pre-predictive environmental consumption plant food export countries can not supply any one of those plant food to them to eat, due to the bad climate to cause them can't grow any one of these plant food to export to sell.

Thus, (AI) deep-learning technology can be applied to predict how to raise the plant food supply number in order to raise price to the import plant food countries consumers to eat, due to they feel difficult to buy these plant food to eat in the bad climate seasonal time in whole year.

(c) (AI) deep-learning technology can help climate scientists to find what reasons cause their countries; rain sudden increases or cause their countries' rain sudden decreases. After its gathering data analysis, it can assist climate scientists to find solution methods to attempt to control the rain level can be right falling down level to let agricultural export farmers who can grow their plant food to sell to agricultural import countries in whole year.

(d) The agricultural export countries' farmers can apply (AI) deep-learning technology to help them to choose whether growing which kinds of plant food in that whether climate time to earn more plant food consumption number more easily.

Due to the agricultural countries climate will often change, for example, tomato, potato, rice, fruit etc. plant food can be adapt to grow in more rain time, but vegetable can not be adapt to grow in more rain time. If farmers can apply this technology to predict when it will have move rain or when it will have less rain to fall down in their countries. Then, they can choose to grow which kinds of plant food number more, in the suitable seasonal climate time in order to raise plant food growing number productivities to supply to sell to satisfy any agricultural food import countries' demand effectively.

(e) (AI) deep-learning technology can help agricultural import countries to solve agricultural food shortage challenge in long term. When this technology can be popular to base applied by the agricultural plant food export countries. It will solve global agricultural food shortage challenge. For example, when one agricultural export countries' farmers can popular accept to apply this technology to predict when to grow which kinds of plant food more to rise number productivities to sell. e.g. vegetable, fruit, rice Besides another agricultural export countries‘ farmers can also accept to apply this technology to predict when to grow plant food, e.g. potato, tomato to raise number productivities to sell. Then, they can concentrate on growing the specific kinds of plant food in order to raise the specific plant food number productivities in every seasonal change time every month. Then, global agricultural plant food supply must be raised, due to these predictive environmental change farmers can know who ought grow which kinds of plant food to sell to raise number productivities.

2.2 How can apply (AI) digital channel to predict consumer behaviors?

(AI) digital channel can be applied to help businesses to evaluate whether how much the product price is the most attractive to persuade consumers feel it is the most reasonable price to sell. It helps consumers to feel which brands of products which ought change the price to let consumers to choose to buy the brand of product. It can be applied to predict whether how many consumer numbers can be increased or decreased when the brand of product's price is variable. It aims to give opinions to help any brand of product manufacturers or sellers to judge whether which price is the most reasonable to let consumers to accept to choose to buy the brand of product in popular.

Thus, (AI) price measurement technology can be preference to be applied online communication ecommerce and mobile phone internet platform aspect. As businesses can enter their past products prices data and past customer number data into computer or mobile. Then, (AI) price measurement technology can gather these data to analyze these product prices and past customer number to compare their prices variable changing range level to find their price variable difference to measure to make conclusion about every product's price variable changing will influence how many customer number increase or decrease changing to choose to sell their different kinds of products more accurate. Then, (AI) price measurement software will help them to analyze all past price variable changing data to compare whether which price range can let customers to feel it is more reasonable and attractive to influence them to choose to buy the product among different brands of product choice.

Because any product's price is one important factor to influence consumers to choose to buy the product, instead of quality, durability, shape, appearance, color, brand familiarity etc. factors. Any online businesses with a focus on Asia should considerate (AI) customer care, and virtual shopping experience, whereas is Europe and North America still value face-to-face and/or real human interaction over (AI) or virtual worlds.

For example, Amazon publish has applied (AI) price measurement technology to help authors to decide how much every different topic of e-book or paper book price, it can attract the largest number of readers to buy. Any one author only needs to type whose book name to Amazon publish author himself/herself Amazon website. Amazon publish (AI) price measurement learning machine will help them to auto-calculate and judge how much e-book or paper book price is the most attractive and the most reasonable in order to increase reader number to buy their e-books or paper books to read. So, (AI) online price measurement machine will gather past similar book names and past every similar book readers' reading times and the number of readers to give opinions to let every author to judge whether his/her very new e-book or paper book ought charge how much price to the e-book or paper book which can attract many readers to choose to buy. Although, it is not ensure that the e-book or paper book price must let readers to feel it is the most reasonable price to choose to buy in reader's view point. However, it has other factors to influence readers' choice to buy the e-book or paper book, e.g. whether the book content is attractive to public, the author's familiarity, the book's page is enough or not to satisfy readers to read etc. factors. But, instead of all these extra factors to influence readers to choose to buy the book to read. (AI) price measurement learning machine can real give opinions to every author to let them to judge the e-book or paper book different price range whether is too high to influence readers to choose to buy to read or tool low to influence readers feel it is possible poor content book to compare other similar content books. Thus, (AI) price measurement machine can help authors to predict every reader's reading behaviors or reading experience and reading habit from online channel in short time easily. The author only enter the book name to let Amazon publish price measurement machine to check, it will follow past reader's reading habit and reading experience to judge whether the similar all book topic sale record to judge how much price is the reasonable price to attract many readers to buy the book.

Hence, (AI) can be applied to digital channel to help businesses to predict consumer behavior in the future. In the future, mobile/smartphone, laptop, desktop will be most frequent used ecommerce channels to develop online business. So, (AI) can be also applied to these platforms to gather data to make analysis to help businesses to predict consumer purchase behaviors popularly. Due to , ecommerce is popular to global, so digital online and instore channels can be one good channel to let (AI) learning machine to make platform to gather past every online consumer purchase (buying) experience data to help businesses to build brand personality and having a responsible, positive impact on society.

To apply (AI) learning machine technology to understand customer online purchase behavior, it will raise business e-commerce successful chance: For example, (AI) learning machine can help businesses to gather data to analyze to determine whether short-term or long-term signals in the online consumer behavior that indicate higher purchase intents to let every online business to know. (AI) learning machine can find that online users with long-term purchasing intent tend to save and click through on more content. However, as online users approach the time of purchase their activity becomes more topically focused and actions shift from saves to searches from online consumption channel. Then, (AI) learning machine will further find that the brand product purchase signals in online behavior can exist weakness before an online purchase is made and can also be traced across different online purchase categories. Finally, (AI) learning machine synthesize these insights in predictive models of online user purchasing intent to the brand of product. Taken together, it's work identifies a set of general principles and signals that can be used to model online user purchasing intent across many online content discovery applications. Thus, (AI) learning machine can help online businesses to gather any online users' click online behaviors data to judge whether there are how many online users will choose to find their online business websites to make final decisions to buy their products from online channels. Then, it will give opinions to help the online businesses to let it to judge whether what are the important website factors will help its online business to attract many online consumers, e.g. designing unattractive website issue, online unattractive product photos issue, unclear website color issue, unclear website advertisement message, contents and words impressions issue, lacking image movement frequent attractive seeing issue etc. different website factors. Thus, online digital channel will be one good choice to apply (AI) learning machine to help businesses to predict consumer behaviors.

2.3 Can apply artificial intelligent learning machine " big data" gathering method to predict manufacturers' behavioral performance ?

In consumer view point, can they apply (AI) learning machine to predict manufacturers' behavioral performance to judge whether whose products are value to buy. Nowadays, (AI) and big data are reshaping the risk in consumer privacy. For example, consumers want to hide their willingness to pay just as firms want to hide their real marginal cost, and buyers have less favorable information, say a low credit shore, prefer to withhold it just as sellers want to conceal poor product quality. So, it implies that it is possible (AI) learning machine can help customers to gather any manufacturers' past sale performance, e.g. how many complaints or appreciation from clients, product quality etc. sale data to let consumers to make judgement whether it is value to buy to compare other competitors. So, it has risk to the poor product quality of manufacturers. Otherwise, it has benefits to the good product quality of manufacturers. It also implies all manufacturers' privacy is not protected or secret when (AI) learning machine is popular to be used to predict manufacturers' behaviors by consumers.

Information economists suggest that both buyers and sells have an incentive to hide or reveal private information, and these incentives are crucial for market efficiency. Data technology that reveals consumers type could facilitate a better match between product and consumer type, and data technology that helps buyers to assess product quality could encourage high quality production.

Thus, (AI) big data technology can also assist consumers to gather different manufacturers' data to compare what their advantages and disadvantages of their products are. Then, consumers can make comparison to choose which brand of product is the suitable to whom to buy in these more choice consumption market. (AI) learning machine will gather similar brand their products' data to analyze to make conclusion to let consumers know or feel to make final judge to find what advantages or disadvantages of these sample brands of similar products' comparison from internet. On the other hand, it means that manufacturers can gather consumers' past purchase behaviors or purchase experience from (AI) big data gathering method to record and analyze to give opinions to let manufacturers to know what reasons or factors influence consumers choose not to buy their products from internet.

(AI) big data gathering consumer behavior prediction method can give these benefits to manufacturers and consumers both, such as: New concerns arise because (AI) technological advance which have enables reducing cost of collecting, storing, processing and using data in mass quantities extend information beyond a single transaction. These advances are often summarized by the big data, it means charge volume of transaction-level data that could identify individual consumers by itself or in combination with the datasets.

The popular (AI) takes big data as in input in order to understand, predict and influence consumer behavior. Modern (AI) is used by legitimate companies, could improve management efficiency motivate innovations and better match demand and supply. But (AI) in the wrong hand, also allows the mass production of fraud and deception. Since , data can be stored, traded and used long after the transaction. Future data use is likely to grow with data processing technology, such as (AI) big data gathering consumer and manufacturer behavioral prediction method from internet channel.

Thus, future (AI) big data learning machine can also help consumers to choose the best brand of manufacturer's products among different brands of manufacturers products choice to compare their past sale performance from internet. They can apply (AI) big data statistic method to gather all different manufacturers' similar products past sale data to compare their advantages and disadvantages to make the best decision to choose to buy which brand of product is the most suitable to them to buy to use. It seems (AI) big data can also help consumers to predict any manufacturers' manufacturing behaviors or manufacturing performance whether they are improving their product quality or are deteriorating their product quality. Thus, (AI) big data tool is also important to help customers to predict future the different brands of manufacturer performance will have improvement in possible.

Thus, I believe that artificial intelligent "big data" gathering method can be suggested to be applied to attempt to predict consumer behavioral changes in global business environment, the reasons are as below:

On the consumer's beneficial hand, Consumers can apply this method to attempt to gather any global manufacturers data to be analyzed by this artificial intelligent learning system. Then, it analyzed all the different brands of specific similar product manufacturer' data to compare what are the range of the best past manufacturing history and sale data to the group of best manufacturers, and what are the range of the better past manufacturing history and sale data, and what are the range of the good past manufacturing history and sale data, and what are the range of the common past manufacturing history and sale data. Finally, the (AI) learning system will compare all the specific similar product, e.g. mobile phone or computer, television, car etc. different kinds of specific products of global manufacturers to conclude the result is such as whether which brands will be the best manufacturers to let the consumer to buy the television or mobile phone or computer or car etc. different kinds of products. It can make more accurate judgement to compare general human's phone or questionnaire surveys investigation method, newspapers, television, radios, internet searches etc. different manufacturing news or data gathering channels to find which brands are the most worth confidence to consumers to choose to buy the specific product in the global consumption market.

On the manufacturers' beneficial hand, manufacturers can apply (AI) data gathering method to predict consumer emotion and buying behavioral changes more accurate. For example, the vehicle manufacturer, it plans to gather data to predict potential driving fast speed sport vehicle consumers' preferences trends in order to make the accurate judgement how to design its sport vehicles to attract many sport vehicle buyers who will choose to buy it's brand of any driving fast speed sport vehicles. It can attempt to apply (AI) intelligent learning system to gather global different brands of sport vehicle data concerns that all past driving fast speed sport vehicle buyer's preference of sport vehicle design. Then, the (AI) intelligent learning system gather global different brands of driving fast speed sport vehicle which had ever been purchased by the different country's driving fast speed sport vehicles consumers. After, it can compare divide the range of similar driving fast speed sport vehicle design and similar price to be different groups. The (AI) intelligent learning system can attempt to follow the past number of different brands of driving fast speed sport vehicle buyers to calculate how many driving fast speed sport vehicle buyers who choose to buy the brand of driving fast speed sport vehicle as well as it will analyze and make judgement to find whether the cheaper price reason attracts the different countries sport vehicle buyers choose to buy the brand of driving fast speed sport vehicle or the attractive design reason attracts the different countries sport vehicle buyers choose to buy the brand of sport vehicle or fast speed reason attracts the sport vehicle buyers choose to buy the brand of sport vehicle.

For example, although some brands of driving fast speed sport vehicle manufacturers' prices are very high, but they can still attract global many sport vehicle consumers to buy. Whether all sport vehicle's attractive design is the main factor to influence them to buy or whether it's fast speed is the main factor to influence them to buy or whether it's safe confidence it the main factor to influence them to buy or it's familiarity brand is the main factor to influence them to buy. (AI) intelligent learning system will attempt to make judgement and analysis to conclude whether the attractive design factor is the main factor to influence many sport vehicle consumers to choose to buy the brand of sport vehicles.

Otherwise, for another example, although some brands of driving fast speed sport vehicle manufacturer's prices are low, but they can not still attract many global many sport vehicle consumers to buy. Whether all vehicle's unattractive design is the main factor to influence them choose not to buy their fast speed driving sport vehicles or whether the unsafe factor is the main factor to influence them choose not to buy their fast speed driving sport vehicles or whether unfamiliarity brand is the main factor to influence many consumers choose not to buy their fast speeding sport vehicles.

Thus, when (AI) learning system had helped the fast speed sport vehicles manufacturer to gather all different brands of fast speed driving sport vehicle's past sale data and price data, design of different sport vehicle, e.g. color choice, method of style, comfortable chair styles and chair sizes and what kinds of steel material to manufacture the sport vehicles data and driving safe and accident occurrence data and the data concerns what reasons of the past complaint to brand of sport vehicle manufacturer from its sport vehicle buyers. Then, it can make more conclusion to give more accurate opinions whether which brands of fast speed driving sport vehicle manufacturer(s) whose sport vehicle design is the main factor to attract consumers choose to buy its any driving fast speed sport vehicle products really. Thus, it seems that it can make more accurate judgement to compare television survey, questionnaire survey to gather data concerns how to design the fast speed sport vehicle to attract consumers to choose to buy the sport vehicle manufacturer's planning sport vehicle products. I believe that (AI) learning system can help the sport vehicle manufacturer to make more accurate conclusion or judgement how to design its fast speed driving sport vehicles to attract it's consumers more easily.

CHAPTER TWO

AI) tool predicts consumer immediate and expected emotion how to influence consumption decision

If (AI) tool can be confirmed to apply to predict consumer behavior, then I can conclude that it can be attempted to apply to predict what the factor(s) of the product itself can cause the consumer has positive or negative emotion, so the manufacturer can attempt to avoid the bad factors cause to bring negative emotion to influence the consumer chooses not to buy the product more easily, such as vehicle product case.

Economists refer to the consumption desirability is as " utility" and the product or service consumption decision making is arose

influenced by maximizing utility only. However, they neglect consumer individual immediate emotion change will also influence the consumer individual consumption decision consequently. Expected emotions are those that are anticipated to occur as a result of the outcomes associated

with different possible courses of action. For example, if a potential investor, were deciding whether to purchase a stock, who might imagine the disappointment who would feel if who ought it and it reduced its price. Otherwise, whose emotion would experience , such as regret if it increased in price, but who does not buy it before the stock rise its price. However, I believe nowadays technology, in the future one day, (AI) tool can be attempted to assist consumer psychology profession or marketing research profession to assist them to find what are the bad factors to influence consumers choose not to buy any manufacturers‘ products. Then, when the

manufacturer
can discover what are the bad factor(S) cause(S) consumers who do not choose to buy their products, then the manufacturer can raise whose product of consumption desirability or " utility" to raise whose product's consumption decision making is influenced by maximizing utility. Hence, (AI) tool will be possible to find what the bad factor(S) to cause consumers do not choose to buy the manufacturer's product in order to raise the product's utility to bring consumer positive emotion to choose to buy its product in possible. SO, (AI) tool will be one consumer psychological emotion prediction tool to assist any manufacturers
to help their products to build positive emotion to any consumers in possible.

The key feature of expected emotions is that they are experienced when the outcomes of a decision materialize, but not at the moment of choice, at the moment of choice, they are only feel about future emotion. Such as consumption case, if the consumer chose to buy the product or consume the service before it's price is increased. Then, the consumer will feel happy and it is worth to purchase or consumer the service as well as the consumer's expected emotion is positive before who decides to buy the product or consume the service, because who believes or feels the product or service's price will be raised in short term, e.g. after one month, one week. Thus, it means that if the consumer does not believe or
feel or predict the product or service's price either it will increase or decrease in short term, whose emotion will be negative, those negative emotion will influence who does not decide to buy the product or service, it is possible that who feel it is not worth to buy the product or consume the service immediately. He She will choose to consume the service or buy the product to wait it's price is decreased later. it seems that the consumer's positive or negative emotion will influence who decides to buy the product or consume the service later or earlier. Thus, it has close relationship between the consumer individual immediate purchase or consumption decision and positive emotion or negative emotion (either expected emotion or immediate emotion influences).

Consequently, if (AI) tool can help any manufacturers
to predict when its product price ought to be increased or decreased in order to attract consumer to choose to buy its product. Then, it can help any manufacturers to build positive expected emotion to attract consumers to choose to buy its product more easily. For example, when the (AI) tool can

predict when the consumer expects the product price will fall down, then it can give ideas to the manufacturer to raise up the product price in the month, then it predicts many consumers expect the product price will fall down after six months. So, the product price will not be fall down after six months. So, many consumers will feel disappointment and they will choose to buy the product if the manufacturer
decided to raise the product price after six months. Then, the higher product price will cause many consumers worry about the product price will continue rise up, so they will prefer to choose to buy the product immediately after six months because they afraid the product price will continue to rise up in the year. Then, I assume that (AI) tool has effort to predict when consumers feel the product will rise up or fall down, then it can give ideas to the manufacturer when to rise up or fall down the product price in order to attract or persuade many consumers choose to buy the product in different period in the year.

1.1 What does (AI) tool predict immediate emotion mean?

Psychologists indicate that immediate emotions, by contrast, are experienced at the moment of choice and fall into one of two categories. Integral emotion, like expected emotions, arise from thinking about the consequences of one's decision, but " integral emotion", unlike expected emotions are experienced at the moment of choice. Such as purchase stock case, the share buyer might experience immediate fear at the thought of the stock's losing value. " Incidental emotions" are also experienced at the moment of choice, such as a consumer predicts the product or service price whether it will be risen up or fallen down. If he/she feels the product or service price will fall down after next month and he/she will choose to buy the product or consume the service. But consequently, after next month, the product or service's price won't fall down absolutely.
Then, he/she will have incidental emotion to influence whom to choose whether he/she ought buy the product or consume the service, due to the product or service price is not still fall down. Otherwise, he/she is fear the product or service will not fall down in short term. Even, it will increase price later. Hence, whose incidental emotion will have possible to influence whom to choose to buy the product or consume the service after one month, if the product or service's price is still not increased absolutely. So, (AI) tool can be attempted to apply to predict when the product price ought need to be raised or fallen down in order to attract consumers to

choose to buy the manufacturers' product in different period.

Economists indicate utility an individual consumption with an outcome might arise from a prediction of emotion: For example, a dinner eater might choose a higher utility to an Italian restaurant dinner than a French restaurant dinner because who anticipates being happier at the former, even the former's dinner price is higher than the French restaurant.

So, such as this restaurant dinner case, if one (AI) tool can assist the French restaurant owner to find what factor(S) cause(S) the dinner consumers do not choose to go to its restaurant to eat its food, e.g. high price factor, bad taste factor, bad wait service performance factor, bad cooker's cooking skill factor, poor advertisement promotion factor, poor familiar factor, poor location or poor eating environment etc. different factors. Then, the French restaurant owner can find methods to avoid the bad factor(S) cause(S) many dinner consumers do not choose to go to whose French restaurant to eat dinner more easily.

The question is that whether the positive emotion factor can influence the consumer changes whose mind to choose to consume the more expensive service or buy the more expensive product. To answer this question. it depends on whether the consumer has an imperfect understanding of whose own tastes or the consumer has a perfect understanding of whose own tastes to the product or the service.

It means the consumer will choose to buy the product or consume the service, even it's price is higher than other general similar products or services if who has a perfect understanding of whose own tastes to the product or service. Otherwise, who won't choose to buy the product or consume the service, due to it's price is higher than other general similar products or services if who has an imperfect understanding of whose own tastes to the product or service. So, it seems that the consumer's negative or positive emotion arise will be influenced by whose perfect or imperfect understanding of whose own tastes to the product or service factor.

It concludes that whether how much degree of the consumer's utility to the product or service. It is not the only one important factor to influence the consumer to choose to buy the product or consume the service. Otherwise, the consumer's imperfect or perfect understanding own tastes to the product or service factor will influence the consumer to arise positive or negative emotion to make final purchase or consumption decision immediately. It will be one more consumption influential factor to lead the consumer to make the final consumption decision making immediately. So, future (AI) tool ought to be innovate to own how to judge good taste or bad taste for any food in order to predict food consumers to choose to buy the food manufacturer's any foods more attractively.

Chapter Two

(AI) tool technical innovation in cruise tourism
immediate positive emotion influence to
cruise travelling consumers

Can apply (AI) tool to cause positive emotion to cruise tourism consumers? Cruise tourism industry is the most influential emotion industry example to influence cruise travelling consumers' travelling entertainment choice. I shall indicate some evidences how it's innovation will influence cruise travelling consumers' emotion to be changed to positive from negative immediately as well as to prove how the cruise traveler higher utility feeling to the cruise tourism provider is not the main factor to influence whom to choose the cruise provider to consume whose cruise journey service arrangement.

Nowadays, cruising has become one of the fastest growing sectors within tourism, cruise service providers need have themselves unique different entertainment service arrangement to satisfy every cruise travelling consumer individual needs in order to attract every one to choose whose cruise arrangement easily, e.g. meals, activities, entertainment and varied destinations create one-stop holiday shop, reasonable competitive ticket fare. Hence, it seems it is one exciting emotion industry. If the cruise service provider can bring positive emotion to influence many cruise travelling consumers immediately. The, even it change higher service fare to compare other similar cruise service providers. I believe it won't influence them to choose other similar cruise service providers if it can often bring immediate positive emotion to its cruise clients during they are staying in its cruises or during they have left its cruises, but they will often remember or won't forget to enjoy their cruise service provider's happing time forever. Hence, if (AI) tool can be attempted to help cruise entertainment providers to arrange different cruise journeys for varied destinations , to arrange different entertainment facilities, to arrange the different taste food to satisfy different countries age cruise consumers' needs. Then, the (AI) tool will assist the cruise providers to bring positive emotion to let every different countries age cruise consumers to feel satisfactory in order to choose to the cruise providers' cruise entertainment service more attractively.

2.1 How can apply (AI) tool to predict cruise service providers bring positive emotion to their clients?

Future, (AI) tool can help any cruise providers to design these kinds of any one entertainment service arrangement to satisfy the cruise provider's customers' needs.

There are different special interests cruising , such as wellness at sea, freighter cruises, river cruises. It has increased the attractiveness of cruising: Romance is for lover cruise traveler target, luxury is for rich cruise traveler target, exotica is for enjoyment exciting feeling traveler target. So, every kind of cruise traveler target will have different kind of cruise entertainment service to satisfy their needs. If the cruise service provider can provide the right and attractive cruise entertainment service to satisfy the specific cruise target. Then, it will bring the positive emotion to the specific cruise target consumers more easily.

Cruise travel was shaped for mass tourism. Prices have been very differently segmented. There are basically four types of markets (Biederman, 2008):

● Contemporary market: On board fun and amenities are playing important role and destinations have secondary importance.

● Premium market: This category is more expensive than the contemporary category and where the destination has same importance as on board amenities.

● Luxury market: It was once dominant type of cruise tourism, but now it has only a small portion of the industry. Generally, it is the most expensive cruise category and usually it takes longer than average cruise days.

● Adventure/exploration: It refers relatively long cruises with special and exotic places where the destination is the main purpose of the trip.

● European cruise travel: Duration takes more five days than worth American travel duration. There is a tendency on European market during the years that duration of travel is getting shorter. This short demand of is explained with the strong demand of customers (Hensen, 2003). Beside this, it is most likely that cruise companies try to convince tourists with short haul travels instead of long term cruise trips for more expenditure.

Thus, I believe that even, the cruise service provider charges higher ticket which won't influence cruise consumers who do not choose its entertainment service on its cruises. If it can arrange the attractive cruise entertainment facilities and destination journey arrangement, staying days arrangement to satisfy different specific cruise target market needs absolutely in order to bring whose emotion to be positive to it's service provision. Then, the cruise service provider will attract many potential cruise clients to choose its cruise service absolutely. Otherwise, if it only bring negative emotion to its cruise clients, it will not attract many potential cruise clients to choose it or loses its old cruise clients, even, its cruise ticket price is needed to decreased in order to raise competitive effort.

In conclusion, I believe that future (AI) tools need to learn how to bring cruise consumers to arise individual immediate or expected positive emotion, this positive emotion consideration is more important to compare to how to reduce cruise ticket price in order to attract cruise clients in global cruise competitive cruise industry.

2.2 Differentiation through the characteristics of cruising route method from (AI) tool route judgement

Future, (AI) tool can attempt to help any cruise entertainment service providers to judge how to design different route to attract different countries age cruise clients' choices to satisfy their cruise journey entertainment needs. The determinants of the cruising route's characteristics (functional, social, and emotion) is important factor to influence the cruise service provider's success. Cruising product is no longer selected primarily for the cruising service, but for the content of cruising route. So, the cruising route will influence the cruise consumer individual emotion, because it is the main service need for every cruise consumer.

The approach called the " land sea cruising in product development" is increasingly becoming an area of interest, e.g. determining the direction of the effects of the individual cruising route characteristics on service value's perception , and providing an evaluation model of the route's perception , and indicating significance variables of attraction.

The questions that cruise planners need to know: How does each of the identified determinants affect the overall perceived value of the cruise route? How the overall perceived value of the cruise route affects customer behavior intentions?

Because different routes factor will influence cruise consumer individual emotion changing seriously. It means the ship has become only a tool, when the offered route whose attractiveness highly influences the impression of the guests has become crucial.

Consumer behavior in cruising segment includes all the activities and influences in the selection of the specific cruise route. There activities result in decisions and actions related to a defined price, selection and reselection of cruising company (Cannot, Brink and Brijball, 2006).

2.3 How to apply (AI) tool to arrange cruise route planning have close relationship to influence cruise consumer emotion?

Firstly, use value of cruising routes is based on the subjective experience, and shows how individuals assess the route during, or immediately after sailing. It is affiliated with the benefits that cruising guest realize by choosing a route , and it is subjective because it depends on the individual assessment (photo taken on the route for one guest presents just a family souvenir, and for professional photographers are embodied financial capital).

Secondly, the utilitarian value is also subjective-oriented and is tied on the point where the inner and us ability of cruising routes are compared with the sacrifice of the client (money and time). Finally, the value is considered as the outcome of the comparison of scarifies and personal benefits, which is resulted in essentially utilitarian nature.

Hence, route design is the main value of cruising tourism and it is primarily determined and analyzed from the aspect of observed customers. Otherwise, the cruise is only one tool to be caught for the cruise passengers, whether the cruise can let whom to sleep comfortable , providing what kind of food to them to eat, what kind of entertainment facilities are provided to them to play, these issues are not more important to compare how to design route to bring them to travel to anywhere to enjoy in this cruise journey factor. Because how to design the route factor can bring each cruise passenger to influence them to feel either negative or positive emotion directly. The whole route journey planning is the most influential factor to influence the cruise passengers to feel whether they ought choose it's service again or not in the future.

CHAPTER THREE

(AI) tool judges the difference between utility factor and emotion to influence consumer decision making

In economic utility or immediate (expected) emotion aspects, whether which is more influential to excite consumption. To analyze whether it is economic utility or immediate (expected) emotion more influential to excite consumption. It depends on the consumer individual consumption choice is in which situations. For example, if the industry's general consumer individual consumption decision is concentrate on emotion influential aspect, such as cruise entertainment industry, hospital care service industry, theme park entertainment industry, movie watching entertainment industry etc. Above all these industries have same nature, it is service. So, it seems that service industry's main influential factor is immediate (expected) emotion influence, it is not economic utility influence. Otherwise, product sale industry's main influential factor is utility.

3.1 (AI) judges consumer utility factor

For this toy choice situation example, parent choose to buy one toy to give whose child to play. They usually considerate which kind of toy is attractive to their child whom like to play. In many different kinds of toys choice, if the child likes to choose the kind of toy to play. After the child's parents had purchased the kind of toy to let whose child to play one period time, e.g. six month. Then, when the child feel that who has need to buy another new toy to play, due to he/she feels bored to play this toy. So, it seems that the child feels this toy has less utility or it's utility is decreased. So, he/she expects whose parent can buy another new kind of toy to let whom to play. It also implies that it is not emotion factor to influence the child to feel boredom and unfunny to play this kind of old toy after six months. It is the product's utility factor which can not attract the child to play it any more. So, this old toy's utility is decreased when this child spends six months to play it. This toy's value is only six month utility to this child to play. Otherwise, if this kind of toy is bought by another parent. It is possible that the another child like to play this kind of toy one year or more. So, it's utility to another child is one year or more period. So, product's utility period is difference, it depends on how long time of the user's satisfactory time.

As this toy case, the child's decision will influence whose parent choose which kind of toy to buy to whom to play. Usually toy price is not difference too much. Parent won't consider when the toy price will be increase or will be decreased to influence their emotion to decide not to buy the toy immediately. So, when the child like to play the kind of toy, even the product's price is more than other kind of toys, and the parent feel it is possible that the kind of toy's price will be fallen down later. They will still choose to buy the kind of toy to let their child to play, they won't be influenced not to buy this kind product by later cheap price factor. So, immediate emotion is not the main factor to influence this parent does not choose buy this toy at this moment. Otherwise, utility factor will influence when the parent will buy another new kind of toy to provide to this child to play. If the child enjoy to play it only three months, after he/she will feel bore and he/she will tell whose parent to buy another new kind of toy to let whom play when the fourth month is beginning. So, it implies that if the kind of toy product can have more attractive utility time, then it can attract many parent to choose to buy it among different kind of toys. Thus, when this kind of toy's utility time is longer time. Then, it is possible that it can influence many parents choose to buy it's different style or design of similar kind of toys to let their children to play. In general, when many parents accept to buy this kind of different style or design of similar toys to give their children to play. Due to it's popular long time utility factor, it will influence children like to play it longer time to compare other kind of toys. Consequently, it will influence parents do not need often spend too much money to buy other kinds of toys to give their children to play. So, longer time utility factor to the product can attract many consumers to choose to buy the kind of product to compare lesser time utility factor to the product. Hence, it proves the explanation why utility factor is the main influential factor to influence the consumer choose to buy the product.

3.2 (AI) judgement tool of Medical care and utility case

Medical care is an input in producing health, it is subject to law of diminishing marginal productivity. Health yields utility to the consumer. It is subject to law of diminishing marginal utility. It bring this question: Does either the patient's emotion or the medical care service or medical care product utility which one can influence the patient's hospital choice more?

To answer this question: We need to know medical care is one kind of nursing care service in hospitals or clinics and medical care product is one kind of medical care product sale from merchants, e.g. medicine or medical equipment. So, in medical industry which has different kind of medical care services to provide to patients in hospitals or clinics as well as which has different kind of medical care products sale, e.g. medicine or wheelchairs, heart health measurement equipment etc. different medical care products in medical health industry.

In medical care aspect, it is one kind of any medical care service to patients from hospitals or clinics. So, medical care is an input in producing health service to patients from hospitals or clinics. When the patient is admitting to hospital or clinic, who needs to see doctor and the doctor need to give the right medicine to the patient to eat to ill whose illness. Even, if the doctor feels the patient whom needs to live hospital for one time period. Then, the hospital nurses must need to take care the patient during he/she is living in the hospital period. Consequently, if the patent can be health in short time, e.g. within one week leaving time, then he/she will be shortened time to leave the hospital in next weak. Otherwise, if the patent can not be health in short time, e.g. within on week, then he/she needs to live the hospital more than one week, even, one month, three months or more. So, the staying hospital time will influence the patent's emotion to feel whether the doctor's effort. If he/she needs to live the hospital long time, he/she will bring negative emotion to feel the doctor's medical effort is not good. The doctor's medical effort can not achieve or satisfy whose expected emotion during whose staying hospital time.

Thus, medical care is an input service in producing health, it is subject to law of diminishing marginal productivity. When the patient does not need to live the hospital longer time, the patient will feel more satisfactory to the hospital's doctor and nurses' care effort as well as the patient can give less money to spend the expenditure to live the hospital. So, the law of diminishing marginal health productivity will explain the hospital will shorten time to the staying days of the hospital to the patent as well as the patient's care expenditure will be decreased when he/she only needs to live to the hospital in short time. Otherwise, the patient needs to live longer time in the hospital, it means that the diminishing marginal health productivity to the hospital, the patient's staying hospital days will be increased and the patient's medical expenditure to the hospital will also be increased. It will bring negative emotion to patient and why this negative emotion factor will influence the patient would choose another hospital to live or find other doctors to see if he/she felt illness in future one day.

In medical care product aspect, health yields utility to the consumer. It is subject to law of diminishing marginal utility. Because patient needs to buy different kind of medical equipment to use or medicine to eat to attempt to cure whose illnesses. So, if the patent can choose the right medicine to eat from the doctor's recommendation or if the patent can choose the right medical equipment to use from the doctor's recommendation. When the patient buy less number of medicine to eat, then he/she can be health or when he/she buy the medical equipment to use, then he/she can be health. Then, he/she will spend less money to buy medicine to eat or medical equipment to use and he/she can be health in short time. Then, the medical consumer will feel the medicine or medical equipment has good utility to satisfy whose medical needs. So, good medicine and good medical equipment can only need short time and less money to let the medical patient to be health.

3.3 Immediate (expected) emotion factor

As cruise entertainment case, every cruise journey must provide fixed stay days on the cruise to let every cruise passenger to play to every cruise journey. So, cruise passenger can not change or extend whose fixed stay day choice in every cruise journey, when they had caught the cruise to go to sea on the day. Is implies that cruise entertainment has none longer time utility factor which can influence each cruise passenger's choice to each different design of cruise journey arrangement.

If the cruise passenger feels very satisfactory and enjoyable to the last time of specific cruise journey arrangement, e.g. five days and four nights New Zealand and Australia cruise journey. Due to this cruise journey can bring positive emotion to let the cruise passenger to let whom feel that he/she can not forget or remember this happy cruise journey forever.

It is possible that this time happy five days and four nights New Zealand and Australia cruise journey will bring positive emotion to influence this cruise passenger to choose to find this cruise service provider to help whom to arrange this same cruise journey or another similar cruise journey again after one month, or three month, or six month or one year or more. Due to this cruse passenger felt this cruise service providers' cruise journey design arrangement can satisfy whose needs and it can achieve whose expected emotion to be positive. So, this cruise entertainment industry must be immediate (expected) emotion influential factor more than time utility factor to influence the cruise consumer's cruise service provider and cruise journey choices.

In conclusion, it is not only utility factor can influence consumption decision. It is emotion factor can also influence consumption decision. It depends on situations whether the consumer is choosing to buy one product or consume one service. If the consumer is choosing to buy one product, how long time of the product's utility factor which will influence the consumer choose to buy which product. If the consumer feels the product can give longer utility time among other similar products, then he/she will have more chance to choose to buy the product. Otherwise, if the consumer feels the product can give lesser utility time among other similar products, then he/she will have less chance to choose to buy the product. If the consumer is choosing to consume one service, emotion factor will influence the consumer choose to find which service provider to consume the same service or similar service. If the service provider can provide excellent service to the consumer, then it will bring positive immediate or expected emotion to whom and it can attract the consumer to choose the service provider again. Otherwise, if the service provider can not provide excellent service to the consumer, then will bring negative immediate or expected emotion to whom and it can not attract the consumer to choose the service provider again.

CHAPTER FOUR

Why and how (AI) judgement tool can judgement what utility factors are to influence consumer emotion

In emotion and utility both aspects, they include these situations. I shall explain how and why emotion and utility factors can influence consumption behaviors in these different situations as below:

(1) In the first situation is brand factor, the brand image, product quality, product knowledge , attitude and

(2) brand loyalty intangible factor will attract the consumer individual purchase.

For example, luxury

products, e.g. luxury fashion brands of clothing. Brands like Zara from Spain and H&M from Seweden began to produce catwalk-style fashion at low cost offering consumers of luxury fashion alternatives at low prices.

Nowadays, the luxury fashion sector is the fourth largest revenue generator in France, and one of the most remarkable sectors in Italy, Spain , the USA and the potential markets of China, Russia and India. The luxury industry has increased having a huge youth in demand. The luxury consumer have much choice in products, shopping channels and pricing of luxury products. It has possible relationship of age, gender, income and other demographic factors with purchasing intentions to influence the rational and emotional buying behavior regarding luxury fashion products.

(2) The second situation concerns the decision-making of make or female consumers are possible experience an emotional desires and

cognitive (reasoning) mind in purchasing choice process. Their emotion includes negative or positive buying emotion and mood management and cognitive process components include cognitive deliberation, planning buying with the exception regard for the future.

University had been using analysis of variances tests, male and female students were found significantly different with respect
affective process components including positive buying emotion, and mood management and cognitive process components include planning buying.

Significant differences were also found between the following product categories: shirts/sweaters, skirts, coats, underwear, accessories, shoes, electronic hardware, computer software, music , CD or DVDs, sports, memorabilia, health /beauty products and magazines/books for pleasure reading. No differences were found in regard to suits/business wear and entertainments.

The investigate proved that some products will have different emotion influence to cause female or male students whose final consumption decision to buy the kind of product. So, the difference od male and female students will have emotion influence to make purchase decision to buy the product in consuming choice process.

(3) The third situation concerns search advertising factor, e.g. online search to influence consumption behavior. Advertising is possible one method to persuade the consumer to choose to buy the product, even the consumer does not know the product exists. For example, proper cloth, a company based in New York, has a site on the social networking site Facebook.

Whenever the company posts a new photos of its clothes, all its face book " fans" automatically receive the information on their own face book pages. "We want to hear what our customers have to say." It seems online advertisement is a potential promotion method to promote any new attractive products to sell to let publicity to know to buy. Internet is one popular communication tool to be used by youth today. So, when one company can have one website to let any youth to find and enter to the website to discover any new things easily. It will cause many consumption chances to let online potential clients to attempt to choose any products to make purchase decision from online advertising tool easily.

How does the role of advertising influence the purchase decision process? Needs and motivations are the starting points of purchase decisions. In fact, advertising is a communication of photo image, sound image, and word advertisement image channel to persuade consumers to choose to buy the brand of product or consume the brand of service between the merchant and its consumers from television, radio, newspapers, magazine, movie etc. channels.

Why does advertisement influence consumer

choice? For this case example, when one buyer waits until more information is gathered before making a decision. The time, two types of cost are involved. First, there are psychological opportunity costs experienced by consumers who are deprived of the product who need and are consequently in a state of psychological tension.

As time elapses, this psychological tension becomes more frustration. Second, buyers experience costs with the information-gathering efforts. They must invest time and energy to visit several retailers, seek out and read advertisements, or inquire for other opinions about the best product to buy.

These delayed decision costs considerably increase as time elapses. The buyer must seek information until it is felt that a search for additional information will bring about more costs than benefits. So, an advertisement is reaching a potential buyer when who is seeking information will have a greater impact, since the buyer is spending time and effort needed to seek out this information himself and he is less likely to find other competing and advertisements to obtain the additional information.

In general, buyers are generally more responsive to different brand advertisements, when they are seeking information on these brands. This is why the becomes a choice target for the advertiser provided the advertiser can identify and locate them. Thus, a client has interested and is in an information-gathering stage is asked.

Then, the advertiser takes advantage of the consumer's having identified him or herself to send a series of informative and persuasive messages or to send a salesperson who will try to conclude a sale. Thus, advertisement gives a chance to let consumers to gather information to choose the best product to buy or the most excellent service to consume.

What of situations do merchants need advertisements promotion? The short purchase cycle markets are characterized by routine

purchase decision processes or by limited problem solving when a new brand is introduced on the market, e.g. coffee, bread , sugar, soft drinks, canned vegetables and household and beauty care products fall into this category. Another irregular purchase cycle markets are characterized by products that are purchased more or less regularly , e.g. cookies, cake mixes, wines, food products. Finally, long or unpredictable purchase cycle markets include all durable products, such as cars, household appliances and furniture (products from which occasions of purchase can't be predicted, which most consumers buy only occasionally). Hence, these kinds of products ought need advertisement promotion specially, due to advertisement can build brand image to let consumers to know. Especially , it is a new brand of product. In conclusion, advertisement will be one good channel to let new product to introduce its brand to let clients to remember in minds heart.

Consequently, future (AI) tool needs to learn how to design different kinds of advertisement to attract consumer attention to the product, needs to learn how to find what the bad factor(S) which cause(S) many consumers do not choose to buy the product, needs to learn when the product price needs to be raised up or fallen down in order to bring consumers' positive emotion to choose to buy the product immediately. SO, if (AI) tool can be invented to own itself effort to design different kinds of methods to predict consumer behavior in order to bring their positive emotion to the product successfully, then the manufacturer can earn positive consumer emotion advantage from the (AI) tool assistance for long term benefit to its product.

How can artificial intelligent tools predict travelling consumer behavior in airline and air agent travelling market ?

I believe that applying (AI) big data tool to predict vehicle buyer consumption choice behavior, it is similar to predict traveler consumption choice behavior. In this chapter, I shall indicate how to apply (AI) big data gathering tool to predict vehicle buyer consumption choice behavior. Then, I shall its what its similar points to be applied to predict traveler consumption choice behavior.

Nowadays, many vehicle manufacturers hope their vehicles can attract to vehicle buyers to choose to buy their vehicles. However, there are many different brands of vehicles to provide to them to choose, so the vehicle market competition is very serious.

How to judge their different kinds of vehicle price which is reasonable acceptance to attract vehicle buyers to choose to buy the brand of vehicle manufacturers' any kinds of vehicles, e.g. fast speed sport style vehicles, comfortable and slow speed common cars, for four passengers common small size or more than four passengers common large car size?

How to evaluate the vehicle prices issue is important factor to influence vehicle buyers' choices. Either if the brand of vehicle price is too high to compare other brands of similar vehicle price, it will influence many vehicle buyers choose to buy other brands' vehicles or if the brand of vehicle price is too low, it will influence vehicle buyers feel this brand's vehicle machine quality or safe driving level or manufacturing steel material or speed or not comfortable sitting etc. different factors is worse to compare to other vehicle brands' similar vehicle products.

Thus, if the brand of vehicle manufacturers can predict how to design vehicles which can attract many vehicle buyers to choose to buy whose any vehicle products. What are future vehicle buyers' favorable vehicle styles? Then, the vehicle manufacturer can concentrate on manufacturing the kind style of vehicle products to sell already. It will reduce its vehicle manufacturing investment risk.

How to apply (AI) tools to predict vehicle buyers' behavioral consumption model? Whether artificial intelligent tools can predict automotive buyers' behavioral consumption model and predict future vehicle design trend. In fact, automotive brands and dealerships are facing an increasingly competition when attempting to manually gathering the vast quantities of data required to create customer focused programs that increase retention, ultimately new sales and service automotive business.

Building a based on that client's intrinsic needs and interests to any kinds of automotive vehicles at any given time. This is especially true in the automotive industry where the time span between purchases is measured in years. Because vehicle buyers would not like often to change their old vehicle to another new one. So, their decisions to buying another new vehicle, the time is usually after one year, even longer time. Hence, it seems any vehicles won't be frequent consumption products to the owned at least one vehicle family consumers (vehicle buyers). It implies that why vehicle manufacturers ought need to spend time to predict future vehicle buyer design choice for whole year vehicle buyer number growth because they won't often change preferable vehicle design to change another new vehicle more easily.

Hence, how to predict vehicle consumers' taste or preferable which styles of vehicle choices issues is very important. If the vehicle manufacturers can not manufacture any attractive vehicles to sell easily in this year. Then, it will lose time, money in this year because it won't know when the owned least one vehicle users or non-owned any vehicle users who will decide to buy one new vehicle or change another new vehicle ensure. The different brand vehicle dealers will possible wait more than one year to attract them to buy their vehicles if their styles are not attractive to compare other brands of vehicle competitors.

However, artificial intelligence and machine learning can help any vehicle manufacturers to find solution to solve patterns in highly to solve patterns in highly complex data-sets that are beyond the capability of a human brain, and then building and automatically acting on the customer insights it generates.

Given the automotive customer need for individualized communications, this technology is positioned to become a critical component of any successful vehicle retailer's domestic or/and overseas vehicle markets. How can vehicle manufacturers and retailers use (AI) to enhance their vehicle marketing campaigns? How will (AI) affect their vehicle sale marketing strategy? What criteria would they use when selecting on (AI) solution?

Vehicle consumers today are able to quickly access different brands of vehicle information, research vehicle products and reviews, negotiate prices and compare one vehicle brand or retailer to another resulting of the brands of vehicle customers. At the same time, the rise of " big -data mining", wearable devices that track user's every move and preference and greater contextualization in advertising and social media has resulted in consumer expectations of individualized. Thus, it seems that (AI) tools can be used to gather " big-data" and then they can make human's mind to analyze how to design kinds of vehicles to satisfy vehicle buyers' needs.

As automotive vehicle marketers can apply (AI) tools to achieve messaging strategies to meet the needs of this new generation of informed vehicle consumers, using data from a variety of sources to move from a variety of sources to move from mass- messaging to more personalized messages aimed at particular vehicle buyer segments, e.g. fast speed sport vehicle buyer segment, slow speed comfortable small size or large size of buyer segment. However, when 90% of vehicle marketers believe having a single vehicle buyer view is important, only 6% have achieved it.

However, one of the main issues vehicle marketers are facing the lack of capacity to efficiently sift through and analyze the massive vehicle buyer amounts of data required to create vehicle buyer individualized vehicle customer experiences easily. This is especially difficult for automotive dealers, the long periods between purchase cycles, and the highly considered nature of the vehicle purchase means that each vehicle dealer needs to not only track a large number of potential vehicle customers for an extremely long period of time, but each of those vehicle customers will generate a huge amount of different kinds of vehicle behavioral consumption data as they research their next vehicle purchase. However, by choosing the right (AI) technological tools and programs , vehicle dealers can solve this big data gathering challenge into a major advantage.

For Forrester vehicle brand example, vehicle consumers have more power over the Forrester vehicle brand's reputation than ever before. Mayne, L. (2014) indicated that Forrester calls this new (AI) tools is the " age of the vehicle customer", a 20 year business cycle in which the most successful vehicle enterprises will reinvent themselves to systematically understand and serve increasingly powerful vehicle consumers. To win in this new age, Forrester declares companies must become vehicle customer obsessed and the only sustainable competitive advantage is knowledge and engagement with customers, such as (AI) gathering data knowledge.

Thus, the biggest challenge vehicle businesses currently face is not the collection of a large quantity of vehicle consumer data, but what to do with that data once they have it. Even at a large vehicle data research firm, the data sets are often too big for a single analyze, or even a team of analysts to sort through and draw conclusion from. However, enter artificial intelligence and machine learning , an efficient technology solution that can continuously find patterns in highly complex data sets that are way beyond the capacity of a human brain and then automatic drive action based on the customer insights is generated.

What is (AI) machine learning tool? Machine learning is a type of (AI) that learns from data and is not explicitly program. Think Amazon, face book. Machine learning serves up relevant content based on an individual vehicle purchase behavior and experiences. More simply, machine learning is a computer program that can learn relationships between data, subject those learnings to errors functions, and then learn from its errors. The program in effect, trains itself.

Lee, T. (2016) explained that "Thus, (AI) tools can learn deep a more advanced branch of machine learning inspired by how our brain's nervous function, has also been found to be especial effective in identifying patterns from data."

When this way sound is complicated from a vehicle dealer perspective, the implementation of a marketing program driven by artificial intelligence can take care of these tasks in an automatic vehicle fashion with little to no manual intervention required from the staff at time vehicle stores.

In practice at a vehicle dealership, the program will continue track vehicle customer behavior online, merging that data with any offline source (like CRM or DMS data) and then analyze this aggregated vehicle buyer data set to predict what vehicle customer may be shopping for and what information they might like to relevance from different kinds style of vehicle design photos.

5.1 Why does travelling market seem to similar to vehicle market which can apply (AI) learning tool to predict travellingconsumer behaviors?

Artificial intelligence refers to complex in vehicle market and travelling entertainment market which is very seem to be applied to predict consumer behaviors.

(AI) machine learning that posses the same characteristics of human intelligence and that have all our sense, all our reason and think just like human vehicle buyer who prefer vehicle purchase choice or travelling consumer who prefer travelling package or travelling destination and airline choice. Besides, machine learning is the practice of using algorithms to collect and examine data, learn from it, and then make a determination or prediction about something in the world.

So, it can be attempted to gather data concerns that travelling consumer past travelling destination choice and air ticket price choice and different travelling package, e.g. high, middle, or low class hotel and foods supply and entertainment places choice in their past travelling journeys.

The machine is " trained" using large amounts of data and algorithms that give it the ability to learn how to automatically perform a task with increasing accuracy. Otherwise, deep learning is primarily based on artificial neural networks inspired by our understanding of the biology of human's brains.

Thus, (AI) big data can gather all these past traveler consumption behavioral choice data to make reference to analyze whether how many travelers will choose to go to the specific travelling destination in any time by the past traveler number record to different travelling destinations, then it can gather the past air ticket sale price to different destinations and past travelling package design to different destinations in order to analyze whether it is the cheap airline ticket price factor or attractive travelling package factor or attractive travelling entertainment etc. in order to predict which factor is the most potential influential factor to they choose to go to the destination to travel in different time within one year. Then, traveler agent or airline can collect these big data to judge how to design their package to attract travelers to go to anywhere to travel or what the main factor influence most of them to choose to visit the destination to travel.

For example, travel agents or airlines can apply "Deep learning" breaks down tasks in ways that enables machines to assist them to predict when travelling consumer choice will be changed and why their travelling choice will change and how their travelling choice will change with increasingly complex tasks.

So, such as why (AI) technology can be applied to predict how travelling consumer behavior changes to bring to judge whether anywhere will be many travelling consumers who will prefer to choose travelling hot destinations next year or next month.

Then, travel agents and airlines can gather overall past travelling consumer data to analyze and conclude the more accurate prediction of different travelling destinations to the number of traveler. Then, they can choose how much air ticket price is more reasonable to charge to the travelling destination or how to design the travelling package which can bring more attractive to the prediction number of different travelling destination travelers in order to achieve to raise the different travelling destination number next year.

Thus, (AI) big data machine learning can help airlines or travel agents to solve how to design any attractive travelling package challenge. A travelling package is both one of the most important and carefully considered travelling entertainment consumption the majority of travelling people will ever make in their lifetime at least one travelling time.

It is also a prediction how travelling package will be designed that tends to be fundamentally tied to a travelling person's travelling destination choice identify and travelling package view of themselves. As the same time, travelling consumers' travelling choice changing lifestyles result in changing travelling destination needs, e.g. the country's young travelers can choose to change non-extreme exciting travelling entertainment package from past extreme exciting travelling entertainment package. Due to personal feeling factor in general. However, I believe that (AI) big data can also be attempted to predict when the country's young travelers will choose to change non-extreme exciting travelling behavior.

It is similar to automotive dealers need to remember that vehicle customers and prospects are individual human beings with risk, complex and ever-changing lives factors, these factors will influence every vehicle consumer why who feels has vehicle purchase need, and how who choose to buy the first vehicle if who decided to buy the first vehicle.

It seems that travelling agents or airlines need to remember that travelling consumers and different features or designs are very traveler beings with risk, complex and ever-travelling package attitude personal changing factors in different travel season, these factor will influence every individual traveler why who feels has travel entertainment need, and how who choose to buy different feature or design travelling package if who decide to travel.

The (AI) big data technological travelling customer behavioral prediction tool seems to be the best travelling behavioral prediction tool in the world are those that know every one of different country's traveler need. Their likes and dislikes which style of travelling package, preferences and travel destination changing tastes to travelling destination choices.

The capacity of the human brain, however, limits us from achieving these different type of travel package sales. In this competitive travelling destination choice entertainment environment, (AI) big data machine learning enables platforms to assist the air ticket and travel package sales team by tracking the travelling consumer behaviors of each travelling customer, learning and memorizing their preferences and predicting their future travelling destination choice and travelling package design needs.

Finally, I recommend that for a travel agent or airline travelling marketing platform to make their travelling customer engagement efficient and fully-functional, I should be able to: applying (AI) tools to track every travelling customer behavior across the web, connecting to a society of data sources, CRM, DMS, third-party, web travelling brands, social traveler email, click etc., aggregating and accurately cross-reference data from a variety of sources, leveraging this data to drive insights on a mass scale, as well as on an individualized basis, driving actions and automatically direct travelling customer engagement via multiple channels based on where each customer is in their travelling individual lifecycle.

5.2 Why is (AI) big data gathering tool better than psychological and survey methods to predict traveler individual travel choice behavior?

Prediction travel behavioral consumption from psychology and survey methods.

How to predict travel consumption? It is one question to any travel agents concern to use what methods which can predict how many numbers of travelers where who will choose to go to travel more accurately. I think that who can consider how to predict travel behavioral consumption from psychology and survey travel choice prediction method, but it is better to apply (AI) big data gathering method to predict travel consumer's destination choice more accurate. The reason is as below:

The first reason is that traveller individual travel psychological desire is difficult to predict accurate more than (AI) big data gathering method, it is due that the data is past traveler's destination choice and travel package and ticket price actual data from (AI) big data gathering method. Otherwise, survey investigation is only traveler psychological thinking method. It lacks enough past actual traveler data gathering.

The second reason is that on the weakness of traveler individual psychological thinking view of survey investigation. It has evidence to support the relationship between self-identify threat and resistance to change travel behavior to any travelers, controlling for whose past travelling behavior, resistance to change if a psychological phenomenon of long standing interest in many applied branches of psychology.

Past travelling behavior has been acknowledged as a predictor of future action. Such as travelling behavior that is experienced as successful is likely to be repeated and may lead to habitual patterns. Some psychologists differentiate habit between two concepts, such as goal oriented and automatic oriented both. Although repeated past travelling behavior is addition goal oriented and automatic oriented. Further non-deliberative nature of habit may make appeals to judge and to predict future individual traveler's behavior accurately.

However, repeated one traveler will choose the destination to repeat to travel without a necessary constraint of goal orientation and automatic oriented both. So, it seems that psychological factor can influence any individual traveler why and how who choose to decide to repeat to choose the destination to travel.

So, survey investigation is only the traveler's thinking to answer the travel firm. It is not sure that the traveler's past travel experience is real answer. Otherwise, (AI) big data gathering method is computer gathering method which gather past traveler consumption actual data to analyze and conclude future traveler possible repeated travel destination choice and travel package choice more accurate.

The third reason is that on the strength of (AI) big data gathering method computer statistic view to predict future traveller consumer's destination and travel package choice. It is structural equation modeling is an extremely flexible linear-in-parameters multivariate statistical modeling technique. It has been used in modeling travel behavior and values since about 1980 year. It is a software method to handle a large number of variables, as well as unobserved variables specified as linear combinations (weighted averages) of the observed variable.

5.3 Can (AI) big data gather data to predict when climate will change to influence poor travelling behaviours?

(AI) big data tool can predict the flexibility of human travelling behavioral change is at least the result of one such mechanism, our ability to travel mentally in time and entertain potential future. Understanding of the impacts is holidays, particularly those involving travel.

Using focus groups research to explores tourists' awareness of the impacts of travel own climate change, examines the extent to which climate change features in holiday travel decisions and identifies some of the barriers to the adoption of less carbon intensive tourism practices.

The findings suggest many tourists don't consider climate change when planning their holidays. The failure of tourists to engage with the climate change to impact of holidays, combined with significant barriers to behavioral change, presents a considerable challenge in the tourism industry. In the future, computer (AI) big data tool can attempt to predict when the country's climate change to influence travelers to choose to go to the country to travel, e.g. next month or next half year or next year hot travelling destinations.

Tourism is a highly energy intensive industry and has only recently attracted attention as an important contributions to climate change through greenhouse gas emissions. It has been estimated that tourism contributes 5% of global carbon dioxide emissions. There have been a number of potential changes proposed for reducing the impact of air travel on climate change. These include technological changes, market based changes and behavioral changes.

However, the role that climate change plays in the holiday and travel decisions of global tourists. How the global tourists of the impacts travel has on climate change to establish the extent to which climate change, considerations features in holiday travel decision making processes and to investigate the major barriers to global tourists adopting less carbon intensive travel practices.

It will bring this question: Will tourists aware the impacts that their holidays and travel have on climate changes to influence their travelling decision?

When, it comes to understand individual traveler's behavioral change, wide range of conceptual theories have been developed, utilizing various social, psychological, subjective and objective variables in order to model travel consumption behavior. These theories of travel behavioral change operate at a number of different levels, including the individual level, the interpersonal level and community level. Whether pro-environmental behavior can be used to predict travel consumption behavior in a climate change. However, the question of what determines pro-environmental behavior in such a complex one that it can not be visualized through one single framework or diagram.

Despite the potentially high risk scenario for the tourism industry and the global environment, the tourism and climate change ought have close relationship.

However, (AI) big data tool can be applied to find what factors to influence the time of travelers‘ travelling choices. What are the important factors and variables which can limit tourism? e.g. money, time, family problem, extreme hot or cold weather change, air ticket price, journey attraction etc. variable factors.

Mention of holidays and travel were deliberately avoided in the recruitment process, so as not to create a connection factor to influence traveler's individual mind. However, the dismissal of alternative transportation modes can be conceived as either a structural barrier, in the sense that flying is perhaps the only realistic option to reach long-haul holiday destination, or a perceived behavioral control barriers in that an individual perceives flying as the only option open to whom.

The transportation tool factor will be depend to extent on the distance to the destination. This can also be interpreted in a social perspective as an intention with the resources available where much international tourism is structured around flying. To increase the availability of different transportation modes, tourists could choose holiday destination closer to home.

Finally, also how to predict future travel behavioral consumption. I feel that travel agents need to predict whether any country's random daily variation of weather factor is also important to influence travel behavior. e.g. in weather, temperature, rainfall and snowfall with traffic accidents factors will have relationship to cause travel demand.

Some scientists estimate suggest that when warmed temperatures and reduced snowfall are associated with a moderate decline in non-fatal accidents, they are also associated with a significant increase in fatal accidents. Thus increase in fatalities and temperature. Half of the estimated effect of temperature on fatalities is due to changes in the exposure to pedestrians, bicyclists and motorcyclists as temperature increase.

So, if any countries have rainfall, snowfall and low temperature to cause traffic accidents, whether this accident occurrence will influence the travelers who liking climb snow hills, riding bicycle, running sports who will avoid to travel to these countries' bad weather after occurs. So, why I feel that this natural climate factor will also be one serious factor to influence travel behavioral consumption. However, (AI) big data tool can predict more accurate than survey method when climate change to influence the country's climate to be poor, then it can predict when which countries are not popular acceptable to global country consumers' travel choice next month.

CHAPTER FIVE

How can apply (AI) to provide travelling businesses with better-informed decisions

I shall explain how (AI) big data gathering technology can provide travelling businesses with better-informed decisions to drive top-line growth, deliver meaningful experience for travelling customers and smooth their path along the travelling consumer journey. The widely understood definition of (AI) involves the ability of machines or computers to learn human thinking, reasoning and decision-making abilities.

So, such as (AI) learning machine system can attempt to learn travelling consumer's travel destination or travel package thinking, judgement of their reasons why they choose to go to the destination to travel or why they choose to buy the travel package and learn how and why they make their past travelling decisions from their past travel big data gathering.

A Narrative science study in 2015 year identified that (AI) was being used primarily in voice recognition, machine learning virtual assistants and decision support. This study also highlighted the many branches of (AI) and that techniques and their definition are used interchangeably. It is possible that (AI) can be used to gather big data , then to analyze to help travel businesses to predict travelling consumer travel destination and travel package choice behaviors. For example, one of the most common techniques is traveler machine learning, where algorithms are used to perform tasks by learning from the airline or travel agent whose past all travelers' travelling destination choice and travel package choice historical data.

However, during 2017 year, search engines will begin to find what additional factors can influence past traveler personal travelling destination and travelling package travelling behavioral data into prediction of future travelling customer behavioral results, such as the online traveler (user's) history of travelling data searches, such as anywhere are the most popular travelling locations or travelling destinations and previously captures conservations.

Artificial intelligence will use this past travelling destinations and travelling package information to power predictive search results, e.g. predictive future travelling consumer's choice behavioral processing for where will be their preferable travelling destination choice and how to design travelling package to satisfy future travelling clients' needs.

Predictive search will improve the quality of online travelling search results, and provide new insights into travelling consumers' travelling destination and package behavior and the moments which matter to them. Search will give recommendation into tailored how travelling consumer individual travelling destination choice in travelling decision making process. Several of the largest online platforms already use (AI) travelling machine learning to improve predictive travelling consumer behavioral search results.

For example, Google's rank brain technology adds research by understanding the context in which the travelling consumer has entered it. Over time, rank brain will learn further from user behaviors Amazon's DSSTNE (pronouned destiny) learns from shoppers' purchasing habits and consumption behavior to offer better product recommend actions, which Amazon can offer before a consumer has entered anything into the search bar.

Such as (AI) big data can gather past online travelers' e-ticket purchase transactions to conclude that online traveler's travelling choice habits and online traveler consumption behavior to offer better travelling destinations and travelling package opinions to travel agents or airlines. However, this technology is not independent of human input. For example, Google engineers will periodically retain the rank brain system to improve the models it uses.

For another example, in 2016 year , Apple computer revamped its travelling scene photos app to allow travelling consumers to search for specific travelling destinations in the travelling scene phots, they want to find anywhere travelling destination photos, not just dates and locations. Each travelling photo that an intelligent phone or intelligent pad user takes goes through 11 billion computations, so that travelling scene photos can understand exactly where is the travelling destination photography to let online travelling consumer to feel anywhere they plan to go to the location to travel. So, (AI) learning machine can make online travelling photos more attractive to influence potential travelers choose to the destination to travel after they see the travelling destination scene photos from internet.

It seems that in future, (AI) machine learning will allow online travelling search to evolve even further. Search engineers will deliver refined recommendations to airlines' online traveler e-ticket search users and use less human input to predict travelling consumers' needs from internet channel. For IBM computer example, it indicated 90% of the data that exists today has been created in the last two years.

This huge explosion of past traveler's e-ticket consumption data gives the opportunity to quickly spot and react to the latest trends, fashion and fads among its travelling clients and potential clients. This will allow airline or travel agent companies to better engage with younger travelling consumers, who gain influence access to the latest travelling destination and package trends.

They associate with to help define who they are as individuals. Thus, travelling company brands have to identify and make use of them before travelling consumers move on, but the vast quantity of past e-ticket purchase data available makes from internet channel. This a resource-intensive task. For next example, Lesara, a based online clothes store, uses this machine learning to inform its product decision often gathering information from internal and external sources.

When its trends -spotting shoes. Lesara has a range of over 20 styles and sells hundreds of pairs a day. It focus on giving consumers, the very latest trends allow Lesara to develop on average of 50,000 new items each year. It compared to 11,000 old items each year. Thus, travelling agents or airlines can attempt to apply (AI) big data gathering method to gather all past e-ticket purchase data, concerns where they prefer to choose to go to the destinations to travel and what travelling packages are the most attractive to the travelers to choose to buy. It aims to help them to predict where future travelers will prefer to choose to go to travel or what travelling package they will prefer to choose to buy next year.

For another (AI) big data prediction example, Lesara is one online clothes store, uses machine learning decisions after gathering information from internal and external sources. One of its most popular products, shoes with LED started life when its trend spotting software flagged up a blogger wearing similar shoes. Now Lesara has a range of over 20 styles and sells

hundreds of pairs a day. Its focus on giving consumers the very latest trends allows Lesara to develop an average of 50,000 new items each year, compared to 11,000 for its competitor Lara.
It seems (AI) big data gathering machine learning can help Lesara business to predict what kinds of shoes design or style that shoe consumers will prefer choose to buy in future shoe market trend. Thus, Lesara can predict shoe consumers' taste successfully and it can manufacture many attractive style of shoes.
(AI) machine learning can gather global past shoe consumer's shoe shopping experiences, then analyzes to make conclusion to give lesara recommendation successfully. This will make the experience more enjoyable for shoe consumers and allow Lesara to advert whose different new style or design of shoes to deliver them move relevant messages by understanding the context of the experience.
So, online travel agents or online airline can also attempt to apply (AI) big data gathering method to predict where travelers will prefer to go to travel and how they ought design travelling packages to attract them to choose to buy next year. Hence, (AI) big data gathering technology can conclude how to design traveler agents' travelling package products to be the most attractive to excite many travelers choose to buy their travelling package, due to it has more accurate to predict travelling consumer destination and travelling package choice behaviors to compare human themselves prediction judgement effort, e.g. travelling survey or marketing research, or telephone enquire. It seems that (AI) machine judgement effort is more accurate to compare to human judgment effort in travelling industry.

6.1 Future travel consumption behavior

Can (AI) big data gathering tool predict traveler individual habitual behavior , e.g. renting travel transportation tools ?

Can (AI) big data gathering tool can predict past traveler destination and travelling package choice habit and it can be intended to predict of future traveler behavior to people are creatures of habits judgement of future anywhere travelling destination choice next year or next month or next half year destination prediction ?

Many of human's everyday goal-directed behaviors are performed in a habitual fashion, the transportation made and route one takes to work, one's choice of breakfast. Habits are formed when using the some behavior frequently and a similar consistency in a similar context for the some purpose whether the individual past travel consumption model will be caused a habit to whom. e.g. choosing whom travel agent to buy air ticket or traveling package; choosing the same or similar countries' destinations to go to travel ; choosing the business class or normal (general) class of quality airlines to catch planes.

Does habitual rent traveling car tools use not lead to more resistance to change of travel mode? It has been argued that past behavior is the best predictor of future behavior to travel consumption. If individual traveler's past consumption behavior was always reasoned, then frequency of prior travel consumption behavior should only have an indirect link to the individual traveler's behavior. It seems that renting travel car tools to use is a habit example. So, a strong rent traveling car tools useful habit makes traveling mode choice. People with a strong renting of traveling car tools of habit should have low motivation to attend to gather any information about public transportation in their choice of travelling country for individual or family or friends members during their traveling journeys.

Even when persuasive communication changes the traveler whose attitudes and intention, in the case of individual traveler or family travelers with a strong renting travel car tools habit. It is difficult to change whose travel behaviors to choose to catch public transportation in whose any trips in any countries. However, understanding of travel behavior and the reasons for choosing one mode of transportation over another. The arguments for rent traveling car tools to use, including convenience, speed, comfort and individual freedom and well known.

Increasingly, psychological factors include such as, perceptions, identity, social norms and habit are being used to understand travel mode choice. Whether how many travel consumers will choose to rent traveling car tools during their trips in any countries. It is difficult to estimate the numbers. As the average level of renting travel car tools of dependence or attitudes to certain travel package policies from travel agents. Instead different people must be treated in different ways because who are motivated in different ways and who are motivated by different travel package policies ways from travel agents.

In conclusion, the factors influence whose traveler's individual traveler destination choice behavior The factors include either who chooses to rent traveling car tools or who chooses to catch public transportation when who individual goes to travel in alone trip or family trip. It include influence mode choice factors, such as social psychology factor and marketing on segmentation factor both to influence whose transportation choice of behavior in whose trip. So, (AI) big data can be attempted to gather past traveler transportation tool choice, rent travelling car tools choice or catching public transportation tools choice to predict where destination can provide what kind of transportation tool to attract many travelers to choose to go to the place to travel.

How (AI) big data determine future travel behavior from past travel experience and perceptions of risk and safety for the benefits to travel consumers?

How (AI) big data determine future travel behavior from past travel experience and perceptions of risk and safety for the benefits to travel consumers? Why does individual traveler avoid certain destination(s) is(are) as relevant to tourist decision making as why who chooses to travel to others?

Perceptions of risk and safety and travel experience are likely to influence travel decisions. If travel agents had efforts to predict future travel behavior to guess whether travelers will feel where is(are) risk and unsafe to cause who does not choose to go to the country to travel. Then, the travel agents will avoid to choose to spend much time to design the different traveling package to attract their potential travel consumers to choose to travel. The reason is because in the case of individual traveler's tourism experience, the traveler whose past disappointment travel experience (psychological risk) will be a serious threat to the traveler's health or life (health, physical or terrorism risk). The past safety or unhealthy risk to the country(countries) will influence the traveler decides to choose not to go to the countries(country) to travel again in the future.

6.2 What is push and pull factors to influence any traveler who chooses where is whose preferable travelling destination ?

How to apply (AI) big data to predict individual traveler's behavioral intention of choosing a travel destination?

Understanding why people travel and what factors influence their behavioral intention of choosing a travel destination is beneficial to tourism planning and marketing. In general, an individual's choice of a travel destination into two forces.

The first force is the push factor that pushes an individual away from home and attempt to develop a general desire to go somewhere, without specifying where that may be.

The other force is the pull factor that pull an individual toward in destination, due to a region-specific or perceived attractiveness of a destination. The respective push and pull factors illustrate that people travel because who are pushed by whose internal motives and pulled by external forced of a destination. However, the decision making process leading to the choice of a travel destination is a very complex process.

For example, a Taiwanese traveler who might either choose new travel destination of Hong Kong or another old travel Asia destinations again or who also might choose any one of Western country, as a new travel destination. The travel agents can predict where who will have intention to choose to travel from whose past behavior and attitude, subjective and perceived behavioral control model. When (AI) big data gather past every country traveler number who chose to go to which countries to travel in order to judge where destinations will be the country travelers' travelling choice destinations in the future.

The factors influence where is the traveler choice, include personal safety, scenic beauty, cultural interest, climate changing, transportation tools, friendliness of local people, price of trip, trip package service in hotels and restaurants, quality and variety of food and shopping facilities and services etc. needs. So, whose factors will influence where is the individual travel's choice. It seems every traveler whose choice of travel process, will include past behavior. e.g. travelling experience, travelling habit, then to choose the best seasoned travelling action to satisfy whose travel needs. This process is the individual traveler's psychological choice process, who must need time to gather information to compare concerning of different travel packages, destination scene, climate change, transportation tools available to the destination, air ticket price etc. these factors, then to judge where is the best right destination to travel in the right time.

Hence, (AI) big data can gather past different countries' climate changing data, transportation tool changing data, destination scene environment changing etc. different data to give opinions to travelling businesses whether any country's these above factors will influence about how many traveler number will be increase or decrease in the future.

6.3 Why can expectation, motivation and attitude factor influence travelling behavior?

Social psychology is concerned with gaining insight into the psychological of socially relevant behaviors and the processes. For instance, on a global level bad influence to global warming, it influences some countries extreme cold or hot bad climate changing occurrence, then it ought influence some travelers' behavioral decision to change their mind to choose some countries to go to travel at the moment which do not occur extreme hot or cold climate (temperature). e.g. above than 40 degree in summer or below than 0 degree in winter. Due to the extreme climate changing environment in the countries, it will cause them to feel uncomfortable to play during their trips. So, the global warming causes to climate changing factor will influence the numbers of travel consumption to be reduced possibly. This is global climate changing environment factor influences to bad or uncomfortable social psychological feeling to global travelers' mind of traveling decision. What is individual traveler expectation, motivation and attitude? Tourism sector includes inbound (domestic) tourism and outbound (overseas) tourism both incomes to any countries. According to recent article, a tourist behavior model has been developed, called the expectation, motivation and attitude (EMA) model (Hsu et al., 2010).

This model focuses on the pre-visit stage of tourists by modeling the behavioral process by incorporating expectation, motivation and attitude. Travel motivation is considered as an essential component of the behavioral process, which has been increasing attention from the travel; industry. The economic approach defines "tourism" is an identifiable nationally important industry. It includes the component activities of transportation, accommodation, recreation, food and related service. So, tourism behavioral consumption is concerned the individual tourist's usual habituate of the industry which responds to whose needs, and of the impacts that both the tourist and the tourism industry have on the socio-cultural, economic and physical environment.

However, travel motivation means how to understand and predict factors that influence travel decision making. According to Backman and others (1995, p.15), motivation is conceptually viewed as " a state of need, a condition that services as a driving force to display different kind of behavior toward certain types of activities, developing preferences, arriving at some expected satisfactory outcome." So, motivation and expectancy which has close relationship to any tourist before who decided to do any tourism of behavior.

Some economists confirmed motivation and expectancy which has relations, such as expectation of visiting an outbound destination has a direct effect on motivation to visit the destination; motivation has a direct effect on attitude toward visiting the destination; expectation of visiting the outbound destination has a direct affection on attitude toward visiting the destination and motivation has a mediating effect on the relationship in between expectation and attitude.

Hence, (AI) big data can gather all the country's climate environment change, transportation tool change, entertainment scene change, hotel price and restaurant price change etc. data to give opinions whether the country will attract how many traveler to choose to go to travel in the year.

CHAPTER SIX

What is (AI) deep learning techniques to forecast travelling environment behavioral consumption

Prediction how many travelers will choose to go to the country to travel. It is similar to apply deep-learning technology to predict how to raise the agricultural farming productivity in the agricultural export country.

The (AI) deep-learning technology leads to performance enhancement and generalization of artificial intelligent technology. It influences the global leader in the field of information technology has declared its intention to utilize the deep-learning technology to solve environmental problems, such as climate change.

So, it will help agriculture farming businesses can raise any plant food: vegetable, fruit, rice which grow up very easily if farmers can apply (AI) deep-learning technology to solve environment problems to influence their plant food grow. If the whole year seasonal change is very good and it is suitable for any plant food to grow in farming land easily, e.g. rain is enough and soil is enough for any plant food to grow in the farm lands. Then, fruit, rice, vegetable etc. agriculture businesses will have much beneficial attribution to global farmers.

The question is how to use deep-learning technologies in the environmental field to predict the status of pro-environmental consumption. We predicted the pro-environmental consumption index based on Google search query data, using a recurrent neural network (RNN model). To certify the accuracy of the index, we compared the prediction accuracy of the RNN

model with that of the ordinary least square and artificial necessary network models.
For example, the RNN model predicts the pro-environmental consumption index better than any other model. we expect the RNN model to perform still better in a big data environment because the deep-learning technologies would be increasingly as the volume of data grows. So, deep-learning technologies could be useful in environmental forecasting to prevent damage caused by climate change to influence any rice, vegetable, tomato, potato, fruit etc. different plant food grow in any countries‘ farming land easily.
For South Korea example, over 800 government agencies spent 2.2 trillion Korea won on eco-products in 2014 year. However, green products are rarely purchased outside these agencies. This phenomenon occurs because there is a gap between consumer attitudes and behavior , that is environmental attitude is a major factor in decision making vis-a-vis the consumption of " green" food and services (Jorea Ministry of Environment, 2015).
Therefore, it is necessary to understand those consumer attitude, that will lead to sustainability-conductive behavior and consumption. (AI) Deep learning system can be applied to attempt understand those traveler attitude to environment protection to fly to which country. For example, (AI) deep learning system can attempt to gather data concerns how many Hong Kong people concern air pollution challenge to influence their health, then it can attempt to predict how many Hong Kong travelers do not choose to go China travel, due to the air pollution challenge to influence their health.

7.1 Environmental travel consumption prediction

Recently, many researchers have studied pro-environmental consumption and household indexes as well as suicide rate predictions using messages posted by internet users on Google trend, Tweets etc. channel.
Whether can environmental consumption be predicted by (AI) deep-learning technological internet channel to influence how many travelers choose to go to the country to travel?
How can impact the pro-environmental consumption attitudes of green policies to influence how many travelers choose to go to the country to travel?
For example, Korea scientists estimated pro-environmental attitudes using

search query data provided by Google trend and confirmed through regression analysis, that pro-environmental attitude has a positive correlation with the pro-environmental attitude index. They also explained that environment-friendly attitude of residents plan an important role in policy making. In the past, most household consumption indexed were calculated through surveys, but (AI) deep-learning technological tool " big data" have recently gained research attention (Lee et al. 2016). So, (AI) deep learning technology can attempt to gather whether how many Korea residents who concern environment pollution to influence their eating green food attitude then to judge whether how many Korea residents hope to leave their country to travel anywhere either high risk environment pollution countries to travel or low risk environment pollution countries to travel in the future.

It seems that (AI) deep-learning technology can help agricultural export countries' farmers , e.g. US, UK, Canada, New Zealand, Australia, Japan, China, India etc. they can predict environmental behavioral consumption to any rice, tomato, potato , fruit, vegetable etc. plant food consumers. The beneficial advantages to them include as below:

(a) Assuming they know their countries' weather, when it has less rain to cause drought or when it has more rain in any seasonal time in the year. They can choose not to grow any kinds of above these plant food to avoid loss.

(b) They can make any kinds of above these plant food price raising after their prediction of these bad seasonal time to cause their plant food shortage supply challenge. Because these plant food consumers' demand number is more, but the supply of these above plant food supply number is less. However, due to they had predicted when the bad seasonal time can not allow them to grow these above plant food before. So, they have enough time to grow many these above plant food number in predictive good seasonal time to prepare to supply to their plant food import countries' plant food consumers to eat. Thus, these predictive environmental consumption plant food export countries can raise their plant food price to sell to them. When, the other non-pre-predictive environmental consumption plant food export countries can not supply any one of those plant food to them to eat, due to the bad climate to cause them can't grow any one of these plant food to export to sell.

Thus, (AI) deep-learning technology can be applied to predict how to raise the plant food supply number in order to raise price to the import plant food countries consumers to eat, due to they feel difficult to buy these plant food to eat in the bad climate seasonal time in whole year.

(c) (AI) deep-learning technology can help climate scientists to find what reasons cause their countries; rain sudden increases or cause their countries' rain sudden decreases. After its gathering data analysis, it can assist climate scientists to find solution methods to attempt to control the rain level can be right falling down level to let agricultural export farmers who can grow their plant food to sell to agricultural import countries in whole year.

(d) The agricultural export countries' farmers can apply (AI) deep-learning technology to help them to choose whether growing which kinds of plant food in that whether climate time to earn more plant food consumption number more easily.

Due to the agricultural countries climate will often change, for example, tomato, potato, rice, fruit etc. plant food can be adapt to grow in more rain time, but vegetable can not be adapt to grow in more rain time. If farmers can apply this technology to predict when it will have move rain or when it will have less rain to fall down in their countries. Then, they can choose to grow which kinds of plant food number more, in the suitable seasonal climate time in order to raise plant food growing number productivities to supply to sell to satisfy any agricultural food import countries' demand effectively.

(e) (AI) deep-learning technology can help agricultural import countries to solve agricultural food shortage challenge in long term. When this technology can be popular to base applied by the agricultural plant food export countries. It will solve global agricultural food shortage challenge. For example, when one agricultural export countries' farmers can popular accept to apply this technology to predict when to grow which kinds of plant food more to rise number productivities to sell. e.g. vegetable, fruit, rice Besides another agricultural export countries' farmers can also accept to apply this technology to predict when to grow plant food, e.g. potato, tomato to raise number productivities to sell. Then, they can concentrate on growing the specific kinds of plant food in order to raise the specific plant food number productivities in every seasonal change time every month. Then, global agricultural plant food supply must be raised, due to these predictive environmental change farmers can know who ought grow which kinds of plant food to sell to raise number productivities.

Consequently, (AI) deep learning can gather where countries will have high risk environment pollution to influence health food supply. Then, it can give opinions to travelling businesses when these high risk environment pollution countries will encounter the traveler number to be decreased, due to the environment pollution serious challenge will occur.

7.2 What methods can predict future travel behavioral consumption ?

How to use qualitative of travel behavioral method to predict future travel consumption from (AI) big data ?

I also suggest to use qualitative of travel behavioral method to predict future travel consumption. Methods such as focus groups interviews and participant observer techniques can be used with quantitative approaches on their own to fill the gaps left by quantitative techniques. These insights have contributed to the development of increasingly sophisticated models to forecast travel behavior and predict changes in behavior in response to change in the transportation system. I shall indicate the weaknesses of human travelling investigation methods as below:

First, survey methods restrict not only the question frame but the answer frame as well, anticipating the important issues and questions and the responses. However, these surveys methods are not well suited to exploratory areas of research where issues remain unidentified and the researched seek to answer the question “why?”.

Second, data collection methods using traditional travel diaries or telephone recruitment can under represent certain segments of the population, particularly the older persons with little education, minorities and the poor. Before the survey, focus group for example can be used to identify what socio-demographic variables to include in the survey, how best to structure the diary, even what incentives will be most effective in increasing the response rate.

After the survey, focus, focus groups can be used to build explanations for the survey results to identify the "why" of the results as well as the implications. One Asia Pacific survey research result was made by tourism market investigation before. It indicated the travel in Asia Pacific market in the past, had often been undertaken in large groups through leisure package sold in bulk, or in large organized business groups, future travelers will be in smaller groups or alone, and for a much wider range of reasons.

Significant new traveler segments, such as female business traveler. The small business traveler and the senior traveler, all of which have different aspirations and requirements from the travel experience.

Moreover, Asia tourism market will start to exist behaviors in the adoption of newer technologies, a giving the traveler new ways to manage the travel experience, creating new behaviors. This with provide new opportunities for travel providers. The use of mobile devices, smartphones, tablets etc. and social media are the obvious findings to become an integral part of the travel experience. Thus, quality method can attempt to predict Asia Pacific tourism market development in the future. It is such as (AI) big data gathering tool can give traveler quality opinions to any travelling businesses to make the more accurate where will be the popular travel destination choice next month or next half year or next year.

However, improving the predictive power of travel behavior models and to increase understanding travel behavior which lies in the use of panel data(repeated measures from the same individuals). Whereas, cross-sectional data only reveal inter-individual differences at one moment in time, panel data can reveal intra-individual changes over time. In effect, panel data are generally better suited to understand and predict (changes in) travel behavior. However, a substantial proportion was also observed to transition between very different activity/travel patterns over time, indicating that from one year to the next, many people renegotiated their activity/travel patterns.

7.3 How to apply advanced traveler information systems (ATIS) to predict future travelling behavior?

Nowadays, information can impact on traveler behavior and network performance. For example, when steadily growing levels of vehicle ownership and vehicle miles traveled information has been identified as a potential strategy towards man aging travel demand, optimizing transportation networks and better utilizing available capacity. Toward, this goal to predict further tourist behavioral consumption. Many countries, government tourism development institutes has applied advanced traveler information systems (ATIS) which travel behavior models and high-fidelity network performance models made increasingly feasible through the rapid advances in computer power. Crucial components of this problem domain are the modeling of individual tourist drivers' response to travel information and the development accurate guidance of relevance to real would trip makers. So, this advanced traveler information systems (ATIS) can assist the tourist who like to rent travelling car tools to travel in any countries own free traveler information systems service conveniently. Also, this travel information system can be intended to assist travelers to make better travel choices. e.g. this system can improve the decision making of individual traveler rather than improvements of network performance overall. So, we need to understand how tourists make their travel plans. Also, understanding decision process that lead to booking of the trip is equally important, as it allows of a potential behavior.

7.4 How can online tourism sale channel influence traveling consumption of behavior?

Nowadays, internet is popular, it seems that booking air ticket behavior of using internet is predicted to influence overall tourism air tickets payment method. Tourism industry has grown in the previous several decades. Despite its global impact, questions related to better understanding of tourists and whose habits. Using online travel air ticket booking benefits include booking electronic air tickets can be made from entering any electronic travel agents websites in the short time and electronic travel ticket payers do not need leave home, who can pay visa card to pre booking any electronic travel ticket from online channel conveniently.

7.5 How can analyze activity based travel demand ?

Nowadays, human are concerning the traffic congestion and air quality deterioration, the supply oriented focus of transportation planning has expanded to include how to manage travel demand within the available transportation supply. Consequently, there has been an increasing interest in travel demand management strategies, such as congestion pricing that attempts to change aggregate travel demand. The prediction aggregate level, long term travel demand to understanding disaggregate level (i.e. individual levels) behavioral responses to short term demand policies, such as ride sharing incentives, congestion pricing and employer based demand management schemes, alternate work schedules, telecommuting limitation of travel agent traditionally work nature shall influence oriented trip based travel modelling passenger travel demand indirectly.

Finally, online travel purchase will be popular to influence the number of travel behavioral consumption nowadays. Any travel package products can be sold from websites to attract travelers to choose to pre-book air ticket for any trips conveniently. In the past ten years, the internet has become the predominant carrier of all types of information and transactions. Regarding travel decisions, internet has also become an important sales channels for the travel industry, because it is associated with comparably lower distribution and sales costs, but also because it adapts to high supply and demand dynamics in this industry. Consequently, the travel and tourism industry tries to increase the internet sale specific share of sales volumes. So, internet sale channel has changed travel consumption behavioral pattern and characteristics and travel experience. For example, Switzerland has one of the highest population-to-computer ratio in Europe. It is also one of the most highly internet penetrated countries in terms of use of the WWW on a day-to-day basis, with more than 75 percent of the population older than 14 years using the WWW daily (ICT, 2005).

The reason of booking online tourism may include: convenience, fast transaction, finding traveling package choice easily, more airline seats available. So, online booking tourism will influence the traditional tourism agents visiting of sales and air tickets and travelling package numbers to be decreased. Finally, the online booking tourism market shares will be expanded to more than traditional tourism agents visits sale market in the future one day. So, the travel agents who still use the traditional tourism visiting sale channel which ought raise whose features to compare to differ to online tourism sale channel if these traditional tourism agents want to keep competitive ability in tourism industry for long term.

7.6 What is actively based patterns of urban population of travel behavioral prediction method?

Actively based patterns of urban population. It is a method of motivational framework means in which societal constraints and inherent individual motivations interact to shape activity participation patterns. It can be used to predict one city or urban the numbers of travel demand in the year. It has two elements: First, capability constraints refer to constraints are imposed by biological needs, such as eating and sleeping and/or resources, such as income, availability of cars etc. to undertake the urban or city's family activities in the year. Second, coupling constraints define where, when and the duration of planning activities that are to be pursued with other individuals. So, this method needs to gather information (data) to get the relationship between activities, travel and spending work time and space time to evaluate whether there are how many families who have real needs to spend time to go to travel in the year.

7.7 What is trip based versus activity based approaches?

What is trip based versus activity based approaches? The fundamental difference between the trip-based and activity based approaches is that the former approach directly focuses on trips without explicit recognition of the motivation or reason for the trips and travel. The activity based approach , on the other hand, views travel as a demand derived from the need to pursue travel activities. So, it is better understand the individual or family behavior basis for individual or family travelling decision regarding participation in travelling activities in certain places or cities or countries at given times and hence the resulting travel needs. This behavioral basis includes all the factors that influence the why, how, when and where of performed activities and resulting individuals and household, the cultural/ social norms of the community and the travel surrounding environment.

Another difference between the two approaches is in the way travel is represented. The trip based approach represents travel as a collection of trips. Each trip is considered as independent of other trips, without considering the inter-relationship in the choice attributes , such as time, destination and mode of different trips. As tours are chains of trips beginning and ending at a same location , say home or work. The tour based representation helps maintain the consistency across and capture the interdependency and consistency of the modeled choice attributed among the trips of the same tour.

In addition to the tour based representation of travel, the activity based approach focuses on sequences or patterns of activity participation and travel behavior, using the whole day or longer periods of time is the unit of analysis. Such as approach can address travel demand management issues through an examination of how people modify their activity participation, for example, will individuals substitute more out-of-home activities for in home activities in the evening of who arrived early form work due-to a work schedule change?

The major difference between trip based and the activity based approaches is in the way, the time dimension of activities and travel is considered. In the trip based approach, time is reduced to being simply a cost making a trip and a day's viewed as a combination, defined peak and off peak time periods. On the other hand, activity based approach views individuals' activity travel patterns are a result of their time use decisions with a continuous time domain. As individuals have 24 hours in a day or multiples of 24 hours for longer periods of time and decide how to use that travel among or allocate that time to activities and travel and with who, subject to their socio-demographic, transportation system and other and scheduling of trips. So, determining the impact of travel demand management policies on time use behavior is an important step to assessing the impact of such policies on individual travel behavior. The final major difference between this two approaches relates to the level of aggregation. In the trip based approach, most aspect of travel, e.g. number of trips etc. are analyzed at an aggregate level.

Consequently, trip based methods accommodate the effect of socio-demographic attributes of households and individuals in a very limited fashion, which limits the activity of the method to evaluate travel impacts of long term socio-demographic characteristics of the individuals who actually make the activity travel choices and the travel service characteristics of the surrounding environment. So, the activity based models are better equipped to forecast the longer term changes in travel demand in response composition and the travel environment of urban areas. Also, using activity based models, the impact of policies can be assessed by predicting individual level behavioral responses instead of employing trip based statistical averages that are aggregated over defined demographic segments.

7.8 Can apply (AI) big data gathering method predict senior age will be main travelling target?

In the past, Germany government had established tourism survey analysis to analyze survey data in order to arrive at reliable conclusions on future trends in travel behavior. To aim to find how demographic change will influence the tourism market and how the industry can adapt to those changes. The travel analysis provided data on tourism consumer behavior, including attitudes, motives and intentions. Since, 1970 year, it is based on a random sample, representative for the population in private households aged 14 years or older. Then, a continuous high scientific standard combined with a national and international users makes the travel analysis a useful tool and reliable source for tourism industry and policy decisions. It aimed to gather statistical data. e.g. on the age structure and on demographic trends, quantitative and qualitative analysis with time series data from the travel analysis. It shows e.g. not only the future volume , quite different from today's seniors, or how who will travel of family holidays will change, e.g. single parents of low, but grandparents of growing significance for tourism.

Demographic change is said to be one of the important drivers for new trends in consumer traveling change behavior in most European countries (e.g. Lind 2001). Because the growing number of senior citizens in the European Union and other industrialized countries, such as the USA and Japan, looks to become one of the major marketing challenges for the tourism industry. United Nations statistics predict that the share of people being 60 age or older will grow dramatically in the coming future, and is expected to rise from 10 percent of the world population in 2000 year to more than 20 percent in 2050 year (United Nations Population Division, 2001). From its statistic, some data showed that travel propensity increased throughout life until the age of about 50 years of age and was then kept stable until very late in life 75 age. The most important results is that the travel propensity when getting older is not going down between 65 and 75 age of course, the overall development of this variable is influenced by a lot of other factors which are responsible for quite a variation over time. It is now possible to suggest that the general pattern of travel propensity is one of the key indicators for holiday life cycle travel behavior, includes three stages. The growth stage tends to increase from early adult hood until 45 age old or when reaching some 80%. The next stage is stabilization from the ages of around 50 age, until 75 age old, starting with a lower increase. Finally, the decrease stage is a slight decrease occurs once people reach the more advanced age of 75 age to 85 age old (Lohmann & Danielsson 2001).

So, it seems Germany government tourism prediction to future travelers' behavior indicated these findings, such as on how future senior generations will travel, who had used survey data to examine the patterns of travel behavior of a generation getting older and applied the findings to draw conclusions on the future. Also, it predicted that on the future of family trips, family segmentation will be the travel behavior patterns in the future. These findings together with the statistical data on demographic change allowed for a better understanding of the coming tends in family holidays. It's aim developed in consumer behavior related to demographic change and predicted what will happen future of tourism one had to consider other influences and drivers as well, for example, trends on the supply side. e.g. low cost airlines or in travelling consumption behavior in general whether how the past may provide a key to predict travel patterns of senior citizens to the future.

Given the projected growth of the senior citizens market, designing specific marketing strategies to meet the prospective needs of elderly tourists will become increasingly important. It has been an implicit assumption that it will be a close relationship between the travel behavior of today's senior citizens and the those of future ones. The growing number of senior citizens in the world. e.g. China, Hong Kong, Japan, USA etc. countries. Global senior citizen tourism market will be based solely on demographic predictions about the future of the population's age structure. However, many of these seniors won't only live longer but will be fitter and more active until later in life. Many of the will also have plenty in life. Many of them will also have plenty of time and money to spend on travel. So, will these new seniors behave like today's senior citizens? Will they adopt the same travel behavior as the previous generation or become a new market of oldies for the leisure and tourism industry? However, to determine the actual number of senior citizens who will be travelling and to sought to evaluate and specify certain difficult to predict the actual numbers of senior citizen to any country. However, they can be based on the implicit assumption that there is a close relationship between the travel behavior of past, present and future seniors. But is this a valid assumption? As the revise- analysis travel analysis survey, which was conducted in Germany every year, offered some interesting data possibilities. It was designed to monitor the holiday travel behavior, opinions and attitudes of Germans and has been carried out since 1970 year, questions in the questionnaire. Data are based on face to face interviews, with a representative sample of more than 7,500 respondents, the interviews being carried out in January each year. All results refer to the average for the defined generated, which ranges generally over ten years. The group of people then at the age of 60 to 69 age is described. This corresponds to the same generation ten years ago, when they had an age of 50 to 59 age. When this methodological approach is not necessarily very sophisticated, it does have the important advantages of being cost effective.

7.9 IS (AI) big data gathering method a better psychological method to compare human marketing research method predict travel behavioral consumption?

On the psychological view point, I think individual traveler's character will have those kind of personal characteristics. First, simplicity searchers value above everything ease not transparency in their travel planning and holiday making, and are willing to avoid having to go through extensive research. Second, cultural purists use their travel as an opportunity to immerse themselves in an unfamiliar looking to break themselves entirely from their home lives and engage. Sincerely with a different way of living. Third, social capital seekers understand that to be well travelled is a personal quality, and their choices are shaped by their desire to take maximum of social reward from their travel. They will exploit the potential of digital media to enrich and inform their experiences, and structure their adventures always keeping in mind they are being watched by online audiences. Finally, reward hunters seek a return on the investment who make in their busy , high-achieving lives. Linked in part to the growing trend of wellness, including both physical and mental self-improvement who seek truly extraordinary and often indulgent or luxurious' must have experiences.

Why needs to know the personal character of individual traveler's characteristics? Because if travel agents could feel which kinds of individual traveler's character, then who can predict which kind of travel package to design to them more easily. For example, how to determine future travel behavior from past travel experience and perceptions of risk and safety? We need to concern that the influences of past international travel experience, types of risk associated with international travel and the overall degree of safety feeling during international travel on individual's travelling experiences likelihood of travelling to various geographic regions on their next international vacation trip or avoidance of those regions, due to perceived risk. Because individual traveler's experience of safety risk degree to the countries, it will influence who chooses to go to the countries/ country to travel again.

Why travelers avoid certain destinations are as relevant decision making as why who choose to go to the country(countries) to travel. Perceptions of risk and safety and travel experiences are likely to influence travel decisions; efforts to predict future travel behavior can benefit to individual tourist's decision making.

As Weber & Bottorn (1989) defined risky decision is as "choices among alternatives that can be described by probability distributions over possible outcomes" (p.114). Some psychologists judge subjective perceptions of physical reality, i.e. image of a particular tourist destination, whereas value judgement refers to the way individual rank destinations according to whose attributes. i.e. attractiveness, safety, risk etc. factors to form on overall image. So, if the individual traveler had unhappy and worried and unsafe experiences to go to where the place(country) to travel during whose vacation time before. Then, this negative travel experience will influence who is afraid to go to the place (country) to travel again. Risk of place, country, destination or region means the danger is relatively high to the place, i.e. increasing in airplane accidents, crime or terrorist activity targeting citizens of potential traveler's nationality or the probability of occurrence is great , i.e. recent occurrences involving travel regions/ destinations under consideration or effective actions to control consequences exist. i.e. selecting safe regions and destinations, taking extra precautions when traveling to risky destinations. These risk factors will influence the individual traveler who chooses to cancel travel plan to go to the country again.

Another interesting research, how to predict behavioral intention of choosing a travel destination, which has focus of tourism research for years, but the complex decision making process leading to the choice of a travel destination has not been well researched. The planned behavior model using its core constructs, attitude, subjective norm and perceived behavioral control, with the addition of the past behavioral variable on behavioral intention of choosing a travel destination.

Understanding why people travel and what factors influence their behavioral intention of choosing a travel destination is beneficial to tourism planning and marketing. Understanding travel motivation is the push and pull model. The idea of the push and pull model is the decomposition of an individual's choice of a travel destination into two forces. The first force is the push factor that pushes an individual away home and attempts to develop a general desire to go somewhere else, without specifying where that may be. The second force is the pull factor, that pulls on individual toward a destination, due to a region specific travel location or perceived attractiveness of a destination. The respective push and pull factors illustrate that people travel because who are pushed by their internal motives and pulled by external forces of a destination. Nevertheless, how push and pull factors guide people's attitude and how these attributes lead to behavioral intentions of choosing a travel destination have rarely been investigated. The decision making process leading to the choice of a travel destination is a very complex process. The planned behavior model is as a research framework to predict the behavioral intention of choosing a travel destination. The model based on the three constructs of attitude, subjective norm, and perceived behavioral control (Fishbein & Ajzen, 1975).

In conclusion, the factors can influence travelers who decide to choose to travel the country, which include personal safety was perceived to the highest motivation factors among the important factors which include, scenic beauty, cultural interests, friendliness of local people, price of trip, services in hotels and restaurants, quality and variety of food and shopping facilities and services. The factors include both push and pull. Push factors include knowledge, prestige, and enhancement of human relationship etc., whereas, the most significant pull factors include high technologic image, expenditure and accessibility etc. For example, Japanese travelers visiting Hong Kong. Push factors are such as exploration dream fulfillment and pull factors are such as benefits sought, attractions and good climate city. It will be the factor of future travel patterns and motivations of sub-cultural and ethic groups for Japanese choice to go to Hong Kong travelling.

7.10 How can apply (AI) digital channel (big data gathering method) predict travelling consumer behaviors?

(AI) big data digital channel can be applied to help travelling businesses to evaluate whether how much the e-ticket price and travelling package price is the most attractive or reasonable to persuade travelling consumers feel it is the most reasonable price to choose to buy the airline's e-tickets or the travel agent's travelling package product from internet channel . It helps travelling consumers to feel which airlines or travelling agents which ought change their e-ticket and/or travelling package price to let travelling consumers to choose to buy the airline e-ticket or the travelling agent's travelling package products from internet channel. It can be applied to predict whether how many travelling consumer numbers can be increased or decreased when the airline e-ticket price is variable or the travelling agent travelling package price is variable . It aims to give opinions to help any online airlines or travelling agents to judge whether which e-ticket or travelling package price is the most reasonable to let travelling consumers to accept to choose to buy which airline's e-tickets or traveling agent's package products more attractive.

Thus, (AI) e-ticket or e-travelling package price measurement technology can be preference to be applied online communication ecommerce and mobile phone internet platform aspect. As traveling businesses can enter their past e-ticket or travelling package prices data and past travelling customer number data into computer or mobile. Then, (AI) price measurement technology can gather these data to analyze these e-ticket or travelling package product prices and past travelling customer number to compare their e-ticket and/or travelling package prices variable changing range level to find their e-ticket and /or travelling package price variable difference to measure to make conclusion about every travelling package or/and e-ticket product's price variable changing will influence how many travelling customer number increase or decrease changing to choose to sell their different kinds of travelling package or e-ticket products more accurate. Then, (AI) price measurement software will help them to analyze all past e-ticket and/or travelling package price variable changing data to compare whether which e-ticket and/or travelling package price range can let travelling customers to feel it is more reasonable and attractive to influence them to choose to buy their e-ticket or travelling package product among different airlines and travel agent choices. Because any e-ticket or travelling package product's price is one important factor to influence travelling consumers to choose to buy the airline's e-tickets or travelling agent's travelling package products.

For example, Amazon publish has applied (AI) price measurement technology to help authors to decide how much every different topic of e-book or paper book price, it can attract the largest number of readers to buy. Any one author only needs to type whose book name to Amazon publish author himself/herself Amazon website. Amazon publish (AI) price measurement learning machine will help them to auto-calculate and judge how much e-book or paper book price is the most attractive and the most reasonable in order to increase reader number to buy their e-books or paper books to read. So, (AI) online price measurement machine will gather past similar book names and past every similar book readers' reading times and the number of readers to give opinions to let every author to judge whether his/her very new e-book or paper book ought charge how much price to the e-book or paper book which can attract many readers to choose to buy. Although, it is not ensure that the e-book or paper book price must let readers to feel it is the most reasonable price to choose to buy in reader's view point. However, it has other factors to influence readers' choice to buy the e-book or paper book, e.g. whether the book content is attractive to public, the author's familiarity, the book's page is enough or not to satisfy readers to read etc. factors. But, instead of all these extra factors to influence readers to choose to buy the book to read. (AI) price measurement learning machine can real give opinions to every author to let them to judge the e-book or paper book different price range whether is too high to influence readers to choose to buy to read or tool low to influence readers feel it is possible poor content book to compare other similar content books. Thus, (AI) price measurement machine can help authors to predict every reader's reading behaviors or reading experience and reading habit from online channel in short time easily. The author only enter the book name to let Amazon publish price measurement machine to check, it will follow past reader's reading habit and reading experience to judge whether the similar all book topic sale record to judge how much price is the reasonable price to attract many readers to buy the book.

Hence, (AI) can be applied to digital channel to help travelling businesses to predict travelling consumer behavior in the future. In the future, mobile/ smartphone, laptop, desktop will be most frequent used ecommerce channels to develop online business. So, (AI) can be also applied to these platforms to gather data to make analysis to help travelling businesses to predict travelling consumer purchase behaviors popularly. Due to , ecommerce is popular to global, so digital online and instore channels can be one good channel to let (AI) learning machine to make platform to gather past every online travelling consumer purchase (buying) experience data to help travelling businesses to build airline or travelling agent brand personality and having a responsible, positive impact on society.

To apply (AI) learning machine technology to understand travelling customer online purchase behavior, it will raise business e-commerce successful chance: For example, (AI) learning machine can help travelling businesses to gather data to analyze to determine whether short-term or long-term signals in the online travelling consumer behavior that indicate higher purchase intents to let every online travelling business to know. (AI) learning machine can find that online users with long-term purchasing intent tend to save and click through on more content.

However, as online travelling users approach the time of purchase their activity becomes more topically focused and actions shift from saves to searches from online travelling consumption channel. Then, (AI) learning machine will further find that the brand airline and/or travelling agent purchase signals in online travelling consumption behavior can exist weakness before an online travelling purchase is made and can also be traced across different online travelling purchase categories. Finally, (AI) learning machine synthesize these insights in predictive models of online travelling user purchasing intent to the brand of airline or/and travelling agent travelling package product. Taken together, it's work identifies a set of general principles and signals that can be used to model online travelling user e-ticket and/or travelling package purchasing intent across many online content discovery applications. Thus, (AI) learning machine can help online travelling businesses to gather any online travelling users' click online travelling behaviors data to judge whether there are how many online travelling users will choose to find their online travelling business websites to make final decisions to buy their travelling package or/and e-ticket products from online channels. Then, it will give opinions to help the online travelling businesses to let it to judge whether what are the important website factors will help its online travelling business to attract many online travelling consumers, e.g. designing unattractive travelling website issue, online unattractive scene photos issue, unclear website travelling photo color issue, unclear website travelling advertisement message, contents and words impressions issue, lacking image movement frequent attractive seeing issue etc. different website factors. Thus, online digital channel will be one good choice to apply (AI) learning machine to help travelling businesses to predict travelling consumer behaviors.

Thus, (AI) big data technology can also assist travelling consumers to gather different manufacturers' data to compare what their advantages and disadvantages of their travelling package products are. Then, travelling consumers can make comparison to choose which airline or travelling agent is the suitable to whom to buy e-ticket or pre-booking travelling package in online travelling consumption market.

.

Thus, I believe that artificial intelligent "big data" gathering method can be suggested to be applied to attempt to predict travelling consumer behavioral changes in global online travelling business environment, the reasons are as below:
On the travelling consumer's beneficial hand, travelling consumers can apply this (AI) big data gathering method to attempt to gather any global airline e-tickets and/or travelling agent's package product data to be analyzed by this artificial intelligent learning system to compare human general marketing research method, e.g. survey, questionnaire, marketing plan etc. different human judgement methods to predict traveler consumption behavioral change model. Then, it analyzed all the different

data to compare what are the range of the most reasonable e-ticket and/ or travelling package online purchase history and sale in order to make more accurate prediction to future traveler change traveling consumption behavioral model in next month, or next half year or next year short term period traveling consumption change prediction. Thus, it seems that future AI tool can be attempted to apply to predict any industries price behavior, e.g. deciding what level of price is the attractive level to attract consumer in these industries, e.g. fuel, education, tourism, health, entertainment, etc. different product purchase. It can give more absolute price suggestion to any merchants to set their price change predict in order to increase many customer numbers to buy their products in every year, or every quarter every month, or month week, even every day etc. different sale period.

Reference

Backman and others “motivation is conceptually viewed as “ a state of need, a condition that services as a driving force to display different kind of behavior toward certain types of activities, developing preferences, arriving at some expected satisfactory outcome.”, 1995, p.15.

Fishbein & Ajzen, “The model based on the three constructs of attitude, subjective norm, and perceived behavioral control”. 1975.

Hsu et al. “A tourist behavior model has been developed, called the expectation, motivation and attitude “ (EMA) model ,2010.

ICT,WWW . “Switzerland has one of the highest population-to-computer ratio in Europe.” Switzerland, 2005.

Jorea Ministry of Environment, “ For South Korea environmental attitude is a major factor in decision making vis-a-vis the consumption of " green" food and services”, Korea, 2015.

Korea Ministry Of Environment. Public Organizations spend 2.2 Trillon Korean Won To

Purchase green Products in 2014; Ministry Of Environment: Sejoung, Korea, 2015.

Lind , Lohmann & Danielsson , United Nations Population Division, “Demographic change is said to be one of the important drivers for new trends in consumer traveling change behavior in most European countries”. 2001.

Mayne, Lonnie. " Evolve of die in the age of the consumer". Entrepreneur, N.P. , 16 Apr. 2014. web of Oct. 2016.

Lee, D.; Kim, M. ; Lee, J. adoption of green electricity policies: Investigating the role of environmental attitudes via big data-driven search-queries. Energy policy 2016. 90, 187-201.

Lee, Terrence, " Tech in Asia-connecting Asia's startup system " Tech. in Asia- connecting Asia's startup ecosystem, N.p.,4 July 2016.

Weber & Bottorn "risky decision is as choices among alternatives that can be described by probability distributions over possible outcomes" , 1989, p.114.

CHAPTER SEVEN

What factors can influence travel behavioural consumption

Prediction travel behavioral consumption from traditional human's mind of tourism market research method

How to predict travel consumption? It is one question to any travel agents concern to use what methods which can predict how many numbers of travelers where who will choose to go to travel more accurately. I think that who can consider how to predict travel behavioral consumption from psychology view and computer science view both.

On the psychology view, It has evidence to support the relationship between self-identify threat and resistance to change travel behavior to any travelers, controlling for whose past travelling behavior, resistance to change if a psychological phenomenon of long standing interest in many applied branches of psychology. Past travelling behavior has been acknowledged as a predictor of future action. Such as travelling behavior that is experienced as successful is likely to be repeated and may lead to habitual patterns. Some psychologists differentiate habit between two concepts, such as goal oriented and automatic oriented both. Although repeated past travelling behavior is addition goal oriented and automatic oriented. Further non-deliberative nature of habit may make appeals to judge and to predict future individual traveler's behaviour accrately. However, repeated travelling behavior without a necessary constraint of goal orientation and automatic oriented both. So, it seems that psychological factor can influence any individual traveler why and how who choose to decide whose travelling behaviour.

On the computer statistic view, structural equation modeling is an extremely flexible linear-in-parameters multivariate statistical modeling technique. It has been used in modeling travel behavior and values since about 1980 year. It is a software method to handle a large number of variables, as well as unobserved variables specified as linear combinations (weighted averages) of the observed variable.

Whether climate change can influence travelling behaviours.

The flexibility of human travelling behavior is at least the result of one such mechanism, our ability to travel mentally in time and entertain potential future. Understanding of the impacts is holidays, particularly those involving travel. Using focus groups research to explores tourists' awareness of the impacts of travel own climate change, examines the extent to which climate change features in holiday travel decisions and identifies some of the barriers to the adoption of less carbon intensive tourism practices. The findings suggest many tourists don't consider climate change when planning their holidays. The failure of tourists to engage with the climate change to impact of holidays, combined with significant barriers to behavioral change, presents a considerable challenge in the tourism industry.

Tourism is a highly energy intensive industry and has only recently attracted attention as an important contributions to climate change through greenhouse gas emissions. It has been estimated that tourism contributes 5% of global carbon dioxide emissions. There have been a number of potential changes proposed for reducing the impact of air travel on climate change. These include technological changes, market based changes and behavioral changes. However, the role that climate change plays in the holiday and travel decisions of global tourists. How the global tourists of the impacts travel has on climate change to establish the extent to which climate change, considerations features in holiday travel decision making processes and to investigate the major barriers to global tourists adopting less carbon intensive travel practices. Whether tourists will aware the impacts that their holidays and travel have on climate changes.

When, it comes to understand indvidual traveler's behavioral change, wide range of conceptual theories have been developed, utilizing various social, psychological, subjective and objective variables in order to model travel consumption behavior. These theories of travel behavioral change operate at a number of different levels, including the individual level, the interpersonal level and community level. Whether pro-environmental behavior can be used to predict travel consumption behavior in a climate change. However, the question of what determines pro-environmental behavior in such a complex one that it can not be visualized through one single framework or diagram.

Despite the potentially high risk scenario for the tourism industry and the global environment, the tourism and climate change ought have close relationship. Whether what are the important factors and variables which can limit tourism? e.g. money, time, family problem, extreme hot or cold weather change, air ticket price, journey attraction etc. variable factors. Mention of holidays and travel were deliberately avoided in the recruitment process, so as not to create a connection factor to influence traveler's individual mind. However, the dismissal of alternative transportation modes can be conceived as either a structural barrier, in the sense that flying is perhaps the only realistic option to reach long-haul holiday destination, or a perceived behavioral control barriers in that an individual perceives flying as the only option open to whom. The transportation tool factor will be depend to extent on the distance to the destination. This can also be interpreted in a social perspective as an intention with the resources available where much international tourism is structured around flying. To increase the availability of different transportation modes, tourists could choose holiday destination closer to home.

Finally, also how to predict future travel behavioural consumption. I feel that travel agents need to predict whether any country's random daily variation of weather factor is also important to influence travel behaviour. e.g. in weather, temperature, rainfall adn snowfall with traffic accidents factors will have relationship to cause travel demand. Some scientists estimate suggest that when warmed temperatures and reduced snowfall are associated with a moderate decline in non-fatal accidents, they are also associated with a significant increase in fatal accidents. Thus increase in fatalities and temperature. Half of the estimated effect of temperature on fatalities is due to changes in the exposure to pedestrians, bicyclists and motorcyclists as temperature increase. So, if any countries have rainfall, snowfall and low temperature to cause traffic accidents, whether this accident occurrence will influence the travelers who liking climb snow hills, riding bicycle, running sports who will avoid to travel to these countries' bad weather after occurs. So, why I feel that this natural climate factor will also be one serious factor to influence travel behavioral consumption.

8.1 Market method predicts future travel consumption behavior

Whether individual habitual behaviour can influence travelling behaviour : e.g. renting travel transportation tools

Whether habit can be intended to predict of future travel behavior to people are creatures of habits. Many of human's everyday goal-directed behaviors are performed in a habitual fashion, the transportation made and route one takes to work, one's choice of breakfast. Habits are formed when using the some behavior frequently and a similar consistency in a similar context for the some purpose whether the individual past travel consumption model will be caused a habit to whom. e.g. choosing whom travel agent to buy air ticket or traveling package; choosing the same or similar countries' destinations to go to travel ; choosing the business class or normal (general) class of quality airlines to catch planes. Does habitual rent traveling car tools use not lead to more resistance to change of travel mode? It has been argued that past behavior is the best predictor of future behavior to travel consumption. If individual traveler's past consumption behavior was always reasoned, then frequency of prior travel consumption behavior should only have an indirect link to the individual traveler's behavior. It seems that renting travel car tools to use is a habit example. So, a strong rent traveling car tools useful habit makes traveling mode choice. People with a strong renting of traveling car tools of habit should have low motivation to attend to gather any information about public transportation in their choice of travelling country for individual or family or friends members during their traveling journeys.

Even when persuasive communication changes the traveler whose attitudes and intention, in the case of individual traveler or family travelers with a strong renting travel car tools habit. It is difficult to change whose travel behaviors to choose to catch public transportation in whose any trips in any countries. However, understanding of travel behavior and the reasons for choosing one mode of transportation over another. The arguments for rent traveling car tools to use, including convenience, speed, comfort and individual freedom and well known. Increasingly, psychological factors include such as, perceptions, identity, social norms and habit are being used to understand travel mode choice. Whether how many travel consumers will choose to rent traveling car tools during their trips in any countries. It is difficult to estimate the numbers. As the average level of renting travel car tools of dependence or attitudes to certain travel package policies from travel agents. Instead different people must be treated in different ways because who are motivated in different ways and who are motivated by different travel package policies ways from travel agents.

In conclusion, the factors influence whose traveler's individual behavior either who chooses to rent traveling car tools or who chooses to catch public transportation when who individual goes to travel in alone trip or family trip. It include influence mode choice factors, such as social psychology factor and marketing on segmentation factor both to influence whose transportation choice of behavior in whose trip.

How to determine future travel behavior from past travel experience and perceptions of risk and safety for the benefits to travel consumers?

How to determine future travel behavior from past travel experience and perceptions of risk and safety for the benefits to travel consumers? Why does individual traveler avoid certain destination(s) is(are) as relevant to tourist decision making as why who chooses to travel to others. Perceptions of risk and safety and travel experience are likely to influence travel decisions. If travel agents had efforts to predict future travel behavior to guess whether travelers will feel where is(are) risk and unsafe to cause who does not choose to go to the country to travel. Then, the travel agents will avoid to choose to spend much time to design the different traveling package to attract their potential travel consumers to choose to travel. The reason is because in the case of individual traveler's tourism experience, the traveler whose past disappointment travel experience (psychological risk) will be a serious threat to the traveler's health or life (health, physical or terrorism risk). The past safety or unhealthy risk to the country(countries) will influence the traveler decides to choose not to go to the countries(country) to travel again in the future.

What is push and pull factors to influence any
traveler who chooses where is whose preferable travelling destination

How to predict individual traveler's behavioral intention of choosing a travel destination. Understanding why people travel and what factors influence their behavioral intention of choosing a travel destination is beneficial to tourism planning and marketing. In general, an individual's choice of a travel destination into two forces. The first force is the push factor that pushes an individual away from home and attempt to develop a general desire to go somewhere, without specifying where that may be. The other force is the pull factor that pull an individual toward in destination, due to a region-specific or perceived attractiveness of a destination. The respective push and pull factors illustrate that people travel because who are pushed by whose internal motives and pulled by external forced of a destination. However, the decision making process leading to the choice of a travel destination is a very complex process. For example, a Taiwanese traveler who might either choose new travel destination of Hong Kong or another old travel Asia destinations again or who also might choose any one of Western country, as a new travel destination. The travel agents can predict where who will have intention to choose to travel from whose past behavior and attitude, subjective and perceived behavioral control model.

The factors influence where is the traveler choice, include personal safety, scenic beauty, cultural interest, climate changing, transportation tools, friendliness of local people, price of trip, trip package service in hotels and restaurants, quality and variety of food and shopping facilities and services etc. needs. So, whose factors will influence where is the individual travel's choice. It seems every traveler whose choice of travel process, will include past behavior. e.g. travelling experience, travelling habit, then to choose the best seasoned travelling action to satisfy whose travel needs. This process is the individual traveler's psychological choice process, who must need time to gather information to compare concerning of different travel packages, destination scene, climate change, transportation tools available to the destination, air ticket price etc. these factors, then to judge where is the best right destination to travel in the right time.

Why expectation, motivation and attitude factor can influence travelling behaviour.

Social psychology is concerned with gaining insight into the psychological of socially relevant behaviors and the processes. For instance, on a global level bad influence to global warming, it influences some countries extreme cold or hot bad climate changing occurrence, then it ought influence some travelers' behavioral decision to change their mind to choose some countries to go to travel at the moment which do not occur extreme hot or cold climate (temperature). e.g. above than 40 degree in summer or below than 0 degree in winter. Due to the extreme climate changing environment in the countries, it will cause them to feel uncomfortable to play during their trips. So, the global warming causes to climate changing factor will influence the numbers of travel consumption to be reduced possibly. This is global climate changing environment factor influences to bad or uncomfortable social psychological feeling to global travelers' mind of traveling decision. What is individual traveler expectation, motivation and attitude? Tourism sector includes inbound (domestic) tourism and outbound (overseas) tourism both incomes to any countries. According to recent article, a tourist behavior model has been developed, called the expectation, motivation and attitude (EMA) model (Hsu et al., 2010).

This model focuses on the pre-visit stage of tourists by modeling the behavioral process by incorporating expectation, motivation and attitude. Travel motivation is considered as an essential component of the behavioral process, which has been increasing attention from the travel; industry. The economic approach defines "tourism" is an identifiable nationally important industry. It includes the component activities of transportation, accommodation, recreation, food and related service. So, tourism behavioral consumption is concerned the individual tourist's usual habituate of the industry which responds to whose needs, and of the impacts that both the tourist and the tourism industry have on the socio-cultural, economic and physical environment.

However, travel motivation means how to understand and predict factors that influence travel decision making. According to Backman and others (1995, p.15), motivation is conceptually viewed as " a state of need, a condition that services as a driving force to display different kind of behavior toward certain types of activities, developing preferences, arriving at some expected satisfactory outcome." So, motivation and expectancy which has close relationship to any tourist before who decided to do any tourism of behavior. Some economists confirmed motivation and expectancy which has relations, such as expectation of visiting an outbound destination has a direct effect on motivation to visit the destination; motivation has a direct effect on attitude toward visiting the destination; expectation of visiting the outbound destination has a direct affect on attitude toward visiting the destination and motivation has a mediating effect on the relationship in between expectation and attitude.

8.2 What methods can predict future travel behavioural consumption

How to use qualitative of travel behavioural method to predict future travel consumption.

I also suggest to use qualitative of travel behavioural method to predict future travel consumption. Methods such as focus groups interviews and participant observer techniques can be used with quantitative approaches on their own to fill the gaps left by quantitative techniques. These insights have contributed to the development of increasingly sophisticated models to forecast travel behavior and predict changes in behavior in response to change in the transportation system. First, survey methods restrict not only the question frame but the answer frame as well, anticipating the important issues and questions and the responses. However, these surveys methods are not well suited to exploratory areas of research where issues remain unidentified and the researched seek to answer the question "why?". Second, data collection methods using traditional travel diaries or telephone recruitment can under represent certain segments of the population, particularly the older persons with little education, minorities and the poor. Before the survey, focus group for example can be used to identify what socio-demographic variables to include in the survey, how best to structure the diary, even what incentives will be most effective in increasing the response rate. After the survey, focus, focus groups can be used to build explanations for the survey results to identify the "why" of the results as well as the implications. One Asia Pacific survey research result was made by tourism market investigation before. It indicated the travel in Asia Pacific market in the past, had often been undertaken in large groups through leisure package sold in bulk, or in large organized business groups, future travelers will be in smaller groups or alone, and for a much wider range of reasons. Significant new traveler segments, such as female business traveler. The small business traveler and the senior traveler, all of which have different aspirations and requirements from the travel experience.

Moreover, Asia tourism market will start to exist behaviors in the adoption of newer technologies, a giving the traveler new ways to manage the travel experience, creating new behaviors. This with provide new opportunities for travel providers. The use of mobile devices, smartphones, tablets etc. and social media are the obvious findings to become an integral part of the travel experience. Thus, quality method can attempt to predict Asia Pacific tourism market development in the future.

However, improving the predictive power of travel behavior models and to increase understanding travel behavior which lies in the use of panel data(repeated measures from the same individuals). Whereas, cross-sectional data only reveal inter-individual differences at one moment in time, panel data can reveal intra-individual changes over time. In effect, panel data are generally better suited to understand and predict (changes in) travel behavior. However, a substantial proportion was also observed to transition between very different activity/travel patterns over time, indicating that from one year to the next, many people renegotiated their activity/travel patterns.

How to apply advanced traveler information systems (ATIS) to predict future travelling behaviour.

Nowadays, information can impact on traveler behavior and network performance. For example, when steadily growing levels of vehicle ownership and vehicle miles traveled information has been identified as a potential strategy towards man aging travel demand, optimizing transportation networks and better utilizing available capacity. Toward, this goal to predict further tourist behavioral consumption. Many countries, government tourism development institutes has applied advanced traveler information systems (ATIS) which travel behavior models and high-fidelity network performance models made increasingly feasible through the rapid advances in computer power. Crucial components of this problem domain are the modeling of individual tourist drivers' response to travel information and the development accurate guidance of relevance to real would trip makers. So, this advanced traveler information systems (ATIS) can assist the tourist who like to rent travelling car tools to travel in any countries own free traveler information systems service conveniently. Also, this travel information system can be intended to assist travelers to make better travel choices. e.g. this system can improve the decision making of individual traveler rather than improvements of network performance overall. So, we need to understand how tourists make their travel plans. Also, understanding decision process that lead to booking of the trip is equally important, as it allows of a potential behavior.

How does online tourism sale channel can influence traveling consumption of behaviour.

Nowadays, internet is popular, it seems that booking air ticket behavior of using internet is predicted to influence overall tourism air tickets payment method. Tourism industry has grown in the previous several decades. Despite its global impact, questions related to better understanding of tourists and whose habits. Using online travel air ticket booking benefits include booking electronic air tickets can be made from entering any electronic travel agents websites in the short time and electronic travel ticket payers do not need leave home, who can pay visa card to pre booking any electronic travel ticket from online channel conveniently.

How to analyze activity based travel demand ? Nowadays, human are concerning the traffic congestion and air quality deterioration, the supply oriented focus of transportation planning has expanded to include how to manage travel demand within the available transportation supply. Consequently, there has been an increasing interest in travel demand management strategies, such as congestion pricing that attempts to change aggregate travel demand. The prediction aggregate level, long term travel demand to understanding disaggregate level (i.e. individual levels) behavioral responses to short term demand policies, such as ride sharing incentives, congestion pricing and employer based demand management schemes, alternate work schedules, telecommuting limitation of travel agent traditionally work nature shall influence oriented trip based travel modelling passenger travel demand indirectly.

Finally, online travel purchase will be popular to influence the number of travel behavioural consumption nowadays. Any travel package products can be sold from websites to attract travellers to choose to prebook air ticket for any trips conveniently. In the past ten years, the internet has become the predominant carrier of all types of information and transactions. Regarding travel decisions, internet has also become an important sales channels for the travel industry, because it is associated with comparably lower distribution and sales costs, but also because ir adapts to hign supply and demand dynamics in this industry. Consequently, the travel and tourism industry tries to increase the internet sale specific share of sales volumes. So, internet sale channel has changed travel consumption behavioural pattern and characteristics and travel experience. For example, Switzerland has one of the highest population-to-computer ratio in Europe. It is also one of the most highly internet penetrated countries in terms of use of the WWW on a day-to-day basis, with more than 75 percent of the population older than 14 years using the WWW daily (ICT, 2005).

The reason of booking online tourism may include: convenience, fast transaction, finding traveling package choice easily, more airline seats available. So, online booking tourism will influence the traditional tourism agents visiting of sales and air tickets and travelling package numbers to be decreased. Finally, the online booking tourism market shares will be expanded to more than traditional tourism agents visits sale market in the future one day. So, the travel agents who still use the traditional tourism visiting sale channel which ought raise whose features to compare to differ to online tourism sale channel if these traditional touriam agents want to keep competitive ability in tourism industry for long term.

Actively based patterns of urban population of travel behavioural prediction method.

Actively based patterns of urban population. It is a method of motivational framework means in which societal constraints and inherent individual motivations interact to shape activity participation patterns. It can be used to predict one city or urban the numbers of travel demand in the year. It has two elements: First, capability constraints refer to constraints are imposed by biological needs, such as eating and sleeping and/or resources, such as income, availability of cars etc. to undertake the urban or city's family activities in the year. Second, coupling constraints define where, when and the duration of planning activities that are to be pursued with other individuals. So, this method needs to gather information (data) to get the relationship between activities, travel and spending work time and space time to evaluate whether there are how many families who have real needs to spend time to go to travel in the year.

What is trip based versus activity based approaches?

What is trip based versus activity based approaches? The fundamental difference between the trip-based and activity based approaches is that the former approach directly focuses on trips without explicit recognition of the motivation or reason for the trips and travel. The activity based approach , on the other hand, views travel as a demand derived from the need to pursue travel activities. So, it is better understand the individual or family behavior basis for individual or family travelling decision regarding participation in travelling activities in certain places or cities or countries at given times and hence the resulting travel needs. This behavioral basis includes all the factors that influence the why, how, when and where of performed activities and resulting individuals and household, the cultural/ social norms of the community and the travel surrounding environment.

Another difference between the two approaches is in the way travel is represented. The trip based approach represents travel as a collection of trips. Each trip is considered as independent of other trips, without considering the inter-relationship in the choice attributes , such as time, destination and mode of different trips. As tours are chains of trips beginning and ending at a same location , say home or work. The tour based representation helps maintain the consistency across and capture the interdependency and consistency of the modeled choice attributed among the trips of the same tour.

In addition to the tour based representation of travel, the activity based approach focuses on sequences or patterns of activity participation and travel behavior, using the whole day or longer periods of time is the unit of analysis. Such as approach can address travel demand management issues through an examination of how people modify their activity participation, for example, will individuals substitute more out-of-home activities for in home activities in the evening of who arrived early form work due-to a work schedule change?

The major difference between trip based and the activity based approaches is in the way, the time dimension of activities and travel is considered. In the trip based approach, time is reduced to being simply a cost making a trip and a day's viewed as a combination, defined peak and off peak time periods. On the other hand, activity based approach views individuals' activity travel patterns are a result of their time use decisions with a continuous time domain. As individuals have 24 hours in a day or multiples of 24 hours for longer periods of time and decide how to use that travel among or allocate that time to activities and travel and with who, subject to their socio-demographic, transportation system and other and scheduling of trips. So, determining the impact of travel demand management policies on time use behavior is an important step to assessing the impact of such policies on individual travel behavior. The final major difference between this two approaches relates to the level of aggregation. In the trip based approach, most aspect of travel, e.g. number of trips etc. are analyzed at an aggregate level.

Consequently, trip based methods accommodate the effect of socio-demographic attributes of households and individuals in a very limited fashion, which limits the activity of the method to evaluate travel impacts of long term socio-demographic characteristics of the individuals who actually make the activity travel choices and the travel service characteristics of the surrounding environment. So, the activity based models are better equipped to forecast the longer term changes in travel demand in response composition and the travel environment of urban areas. Also, using activity based models, the impact of policies can be assessed by predicting individual level behavioral responses instead of employing trip based statistical averages that are aggregated over defined demographic segments.

Why senior age will be main travelling target.

In the past, Germany government had established tourism survey analysis to analyze survey data in order to arrive at reliable conclusions on future trends in travel behavior. To aim to find how demographic change will influence the tourism market and how the industry can adapt to those changes. The travel analysis provided data on tourism consumer behavior, including attitudes, motives and intentions. Since, 1970 year, it is based on a random sample, representative for the population in private households aged 14 years or older. Then, a continuous high scientific standard combined with a national and international users makes the travel analysis a useful tool and reliable source for tourism industry and policy decisions. It aimed to gather statistical data. e.g. on the age structure and on demographic trends, quantitative and qualitative analysis with time series data from the travel analysis. It shows e.g. not only the future volume , quite different from today's seniors, or how who will travel of family holidays will change, e.g. single parents of low, but grandparents of growing significance for tourism.

Demographic change is said to be one of the important drivers for new trends in consumer traveling change behavior in most European countries (e.g. Lind 2001). Because the growing number of senior citizens in the European Union and other industralised countries, such as the USA and Japan, looks to become one of the major marketing challenges for the tourism industry. United Nations statistics predict that the share of people being 60 age or older will grow dramatically in the coming future, and is expected to rise from 10 percent of the world population in 2000 year to more than 20 percent in 2050 year (United Nations Population Division, 2001). From its statistic, some data showed that travel propensity increased throughout life until the age of about 50 years of age and was then kept stable until very late in life 75 age. The most important results is that the travel propensity when getting older is not going down between 65 and 75 age of course, the overall development of this variable is influenced by a lot of other factors which are rsponsible for quite a variation over time. It is now possible to suggest that the general pattern of travel propensity is one of the key indicators for holiday life cycle travel behaviour, includes three stages. The growth stage tends to increase from early aduithood until 45 age old or when reaching some 80%. The next stage is stabilisation from the ages of around 50 age,until 75 age old, starting with a lower increase. Finally, the decrease stage is a slight decrease occurs once people reach the more advanced age of 75 age to 85 age old (Lohmann & Danielsson 2001).

So, it seems Germany government tourism prediction to future travellers' behaviour indicated these findings, such as on how future senior generations will travel, who had used survey data to examine the patterns of travel behaviour of a generation getting older and applied the findings to draw conclusions on the future. Also, it predicted that on the future of family trips, family semgmentation will be the travel behaviour patterns in the future. These findings together with the statistical data on demographic change allowed for a better understanding of the coming tends in family holidays. It's aim developed in consumer behaviour related to demographic change and predicted what will happen future of tourism one had to consider other influences and drivers as well, for example, trends on the supply side. e.g. low cost airlines or in travelling consumption behaviour in general whether how the past may provide a key to predict travel patterns of senior sitizens to the future.

Given the projected growth of the senior citizens market, designing specific marketing strategies to meet the prospective needs of elderly tourists will become increasingly important. It has been an implict assumption that it will be a close relationship between the travel behaviour of today's senior citizens and the those of future ones. The growing number of senior citizens in the world. e.g. China, Hong Kong, Japan, USA etc. countries. Global senior citizen tourism market will be based solely on demographic predictions about the future of the population's age structure. However, many of these seniors won't only live longer but will be fitter and more active until later in life. Many of the will also have plenty in life. Many of them will also have plenty of time and money to spend on travel. So, will these new seniors behave like today's senior citizens? Will they adopt the same travel behaviour as the previous generation or become a new market of oldies for the leisure and tourism indudtry? However, to determine the actual number of senior citizens who will be travelling and to sought to evaluate and specify certain difficult to predict the actual numbers of senior citizen to any country. However, they can be based on the implicit assumption that there is a close relationship between the travel behaviour of past, present and future seniors. But is this a valid assumption? As the reiseanalyse travel analysis survey, which was conducted in Germany every year, offered some interesting data possibiltieis. It was designed to monitor the holiday travel behaviour, opinions and attitudes of Germans and has been carried out since 1970 year, questions in the questionnaire. Data are based on face to face interviews, with a representative sample of more than

7,500 repondents, the interviews being carried out in January each year. All results refer to the average for the defined generated, which ranges generally over ten years. The group of people then at the age of 60 to 69 age is described. This corresponds to the same generation ten years ago, when they had an age of 50 to 59 age. When this methodological approach is not necessarily very sophisticated, it does have the important advantages of being cost effective.

Psychological method to predict travel behavioural consumption.

On the psychological view point, I think individual traveler's character will have those kind of personal characteristics. First, simplicity searchers value above everything ease not transparency in their travel planning and holiday making, and are willing to avoid having to go through extensive research. Second, cultural purists use their travel as an opportunity to immerse themselves in an unfamiliar looking to break themselves entirely from their home lives and engage. Sincerely with a different way of living. Third, social capital seekers understand that to be well travelled is a personal quality, and their choices are shaped by their desire to take maximum of social reward from their travel. They will exploit the potential of digital media to enrich and inform their experiences, and structure their adventures always keeping in mind they are being watched by online audiences. Finally, reward hunters seek a return on the investment who make in their busy , high-achieving lives. Linked in part to the growing trend of wellness, including both physical and mental self improvement who seek truly extraordinary and often indulgent or luxurious' must have experiences.

Why needs to know the personal character of individual traveler's characteristics. Because if travel agents could feel which kinds of individual traveler's character, then who can predict which kind of travel package to design to them more easily. For example, how to determine future travel behaviour from past travel experience and perceptions of risk and safety? We need to concern that the influences of past international travel experience, types of risk associated with international travel and the overall degree of safety feeling during international travel on individual's travelling experiences likelihood of travelling to various geographic regions on their next international vacation trip or avoidance of those regions, due to perceived risk. Because individual traveler's experience of safety risk degree to the countries, it will influence who chooses to go to the countries/ country to travel again.

Why travellers avoid certain destinations are as relevant decision making as why who choose to go to the country(countries) to travel. Perceptions of risk and safety and travel experiences are likely to influence travel decisions; efforts to predict future travel behaviour can benefit to individual tourist's decision making. As Weber & Bottorn (1989) defined risky decision is as "choices among alternatives that can be described by prodability distributions over possible outcomes" (p.114). Some psychologists judge subjective perceptions of physical reality, i.e. image of a particular tourist destination, whereas value judgement refers to the way individual rank destinations according to whose attributes. i.e. attractiveness, safety, risk etc. factors to form on overall image. So, if the individual traveler had unhappy and worried and unsafe experiences to go to where the place(country) to travel during whose vacation time before. Then, this negative travel experience will influence who is afraid to go to the place (country) to travel again. Risk of place, country, destination or region means the danger is relatively high to the place, ie. increasing in airplane accidents, crime or terrorist activity targeting citizens of potential traveler's nationality or the probability of occurrence is great , ie. recent occurrences involving travel regions/destinations under consideration or effective actions to control consequences exist. i.e. selecting safe regions and destinations, taking extra precautions when traveling to risky destinations. These risk factors will influence the individual traveler who chooses to cancel travel plan to go to the country again.

Another interesting research, how to predict behavioural intention of choosing a travel destination, which has focus of toursm research for years, but the complex decision making process leading to the choice of a travel destination has not been well researched. The planned behaviour model using its core constructs, attitude, subjective norm and perceived behavioural control, with the addition of the past behavioural variable on behavioural intention of choosing a travel destination.

Understanding why people travel and what factors influence their behavioural intention of choosing a travel destination is beneficial to tourism planning and marketing. Understanding travel motivation is the push and pull model. The idea of the push and pull model is the decomposition of an individual's choice of a travel destination into two forces. The first force is the push factor that pushes an indvidual away home and attempts to develop a general desire to go somewhere else, without specifying where that may be. The second force is the pull factor, that pulls on individual toward a destination, due to a region specific travel location or perceived attractiveness of a destination. The respective push and pull factors illustrate that people travel because who are pushed by their internal motives and pulled by external forces of a destination. Nevertheless, how push and pull factors guide people's attitude and how these attributes lead to behavioural intentions of choosing a travel destination have rarely been investigated. The decision making process leading to the choice of a travel destination is a very complex process. The planned behaviour model is as a research framework to predict the behavioural intention of choosing a travel destination. The model based on the three constructs of attitude, subjective norm, and perceived behavioural control (Fishbein & Ajzen, 1975).

In conclusion, the factors can influence travelers who decide to choose to travel the country, which include personal safety was perceived to the highest motivation factors among the important factors which include, scenic beauty, cultural interests, friendliness of local people, price of trip, services in hotels and restaurants, quality and variety of food and shopping facilities and services. The factors include both push and pull. Push factors include knowledge, prestige, and enhancement of human relationship etc., whereas, the most significant pull factors include high technologic image, expenditure and accessibility etc. For example, Japanese travelers visiting Hong Kong. Push factors are such as exploration dream fulfillment and pull factors are such as benefits sought, attractions and good climate city. It will be the factor of future travel patterns and motivations of sub-cultural and ethic groups for Japanese choice to go to Hong Kong travelling.

Bibliography

Backman, K., Backman, S., Uysal, M. And Sunshine, K. (1995). Event Tourism : An Examination Of Motivations And Activities. Festival Management And Event Tourism, 3(1), 15-24.

Fishbein, M., & Ajzen, Z. (1975). Belief, Attitude, Intention And Behaviour: An Introduction To Theory And Research, Boston: Addison Wesley.

Hsu, C.H.C., Cai , L.A., Li, M(2010). Expectation,
Motivation And Attitude: A Tourist Behavioral
Model. Journal Of Travel Research, 49(3),
282-296. http://dx.doi, org/10.1177/004728750

9349266.

ICT Information And Communication Technology Switzerland, 2005. ICT Fakten (ICT facts).

Available from http://www.ictswitzerland.ch/de/ict%2fakten/factsfigures.asp(retrieved Dec.12, 2005) in German.

Lind, (2001): Befolkningen, Familjen, Livscykeln- Och Ekonomisk Tillvaxt. Institutet For Tillvaxtpo-litiska studier/Vinnova/Nutek.

Lohmann, Martin (2001): The 31 st. Reiseanalyse-RA 2001. Tourism: vol. 49, no.1/2001;pp.65-67, Zagreb.

United Nations Population Division (2001). World Population Prospects: The 2000 year Revision, New York.

Weber E.U., & W, P.Bottom (1989). "Axiomatic

Measures Of Perceived Risk: Some Tests And extensions." journal of behavioral decision making, 2 (2): 113-31.

CHAPTER EIGHT

Main barriers influence artificial intelligence consumer behavioral prediction

In future, it is possible that these barriers will influence how to apply (AI technology) to predict consumer behavior in success. The barriers may include: Lacking of a (AI) digital data gathering vision and strategy, lacking of efficient workforce readiness, (AI) technology constraints., non reaching (AI) consumer behavioral prediction mature stage, time and money and resource constraints, law and regulations prohibition to develop (AI) consumer behavioral prediction bug data gather technology.

However, the recommendation of solutions to attack the barriers to influence artificial intelligence consumer behavioral prediction not success, it may include gaining employee buy in to participate and develop (AI) consumer behavioral prediction technology, making customer experience to a concern (AI) big data gather questionnaire investigation, providing compensation, training to employees in order to achieve (AI) consumer behavioral big data questionnaire investigation research digital technological goals and strategy, task senior leaders manage any (AI) digital big data gather technology changes, putting policies and (AI) big data gather digital technology in place to support a fully remote, flexible workforce in any (AI) digital big data gather questionnaires research projects, teaching all employees how to code/understand (AI) big data gather consumer behavioral prediction software development, appointing a chief (AI) officer to manage any (AI) big data gather customer behavioral prediction projects and automate everything and encourage customers to attempt experience to self-service and (AI) big data gather questionnaire research to earn beneficial consumption aim after they gave feedback to any (AI) digital questionnaire researches. So, in the future, the (AI) digital big data questionnaire researches can include these industries surveyed, such as automat m financial services, public healthcare, private healthcare, technology, telecoms, insurance, life sciences, manufacturing, media and entertainment , oil and gas, retail and consumer products etc.

Hence, in the future, any of these industries can attempt to apply (AI) digital big data gather technology to predict how and why consumer behaviors will change in order to avoid reducing consumer number threat occurrence.

6.1 (AI) digital data gather technology predicts food consumer behavior's main barriers

What are the main barriers to food industry? When the food manufacturer applies (AI) big data gather technology to predict food consumer behavior? The barriers include that the food manufacturer / provider needs to decide whether when the right time is applied to the right (AI) digital big data prediction tool channel to find the right food consumers to be chose to full food consumption satisfactory questionnaires, how to gather multi-class food consumption classifiers on real-world food consumers transactional data from the food sale domain consistently to show the critical numbers of different kinds of food items at which the predictive performance most accurate? So, any food manufacturer / provider's advanced in (AI) digital data gather warehousing and management technologies can provide that opportunities for food business to enhance long term relationship with the food providers' clients.

However, food industry's (AI) digital data gather aims to improve food customer product targeting, increase food customer loyalty and food purchase probability to the food supplier. To effective identify, understand and satisfy the needs of their food customers, the food suppliers need to develop the right (AI) digital questionnaire questions and find the right food customers to fill every right questions from every digital questionnaire at the right time through the right channel.

Above of all these, they will be the barriers when one food supplier expects its (AI) digital data gather questionnaires which can conclude the most accurate prediction concerns any kinds of consumer food product choices. So, such as (AI) digital data prediction model, it is needed to incorporate into the food market segmentation, food customer targeting, and food challenging decisions with the goal of maximizing the total food customer lifetime. For example, (AI) big data gather transaction data is reasonable and accurate for building predictive models. Transaction data can be electronically collected and readily made available for data mining in lot quantity at minimum extra costs.

Suggestion to apply (AI) prototypes of food customer profiles method to predict food customer behavioral changes. Prototypes of food customer profiles mean to be extracted from the discovered bins and multi-class classifies models are built using those prototypes. The learned models can than be used to predict the class of food customer profiles (e.g. restaurants, school canteens, supermarkets etc. food suppliers) based on their food purchases. The approach is validated on the case study of a food retail and food service company operating in food and beverages market.

So, a food customer profile, it is a description (AI) data gather tool will record every of food customer using available information, which help in understanding their background and food consumption behavior. (AI) data gather tool can well develop every food customer profile, every food customer data is essential in food market analysis as they aid food suppliers in saving time and money by highlighting the real potential food consumers whose needs are to be met rather a range of individuals.

So, (AI) data gather tool can record every food consumer profile and every can be factual or behavioral food consumption. A factual food customer profile consists of a set of characteristics for (AI) big data gather record, e.g. demographic information , such as food customer name, gender, birth date, when a behavioral food customer profile consists of what the food customer is actually doing and is usually derived from (AI) digital transactional data gather record.

So, (AI) big data gather record's every behavioral food consumer profile can be much stronger predictor of the future food supplier consumption choice actions of a food customer. Furthermore, the food supplier's (AI) all past food consumer information that make up demographically based all past food customer profiles are expensive to acquire when the information for the food suppliers' past every food consumer food consumption behaviors. Moreover, food customer profile can be recorded to make real food purchase every time. So, when the food supplier finds the past food consumer's record from (AI) big data gather tool. Then, it can make more accurate judgement whether past every food consumer has chose to buy its food to eat how many times every year in order to predict whether its every past food consumer will choose to buy its foods how many times next year in possible. If the next year, its every past food consumer's consumption time to the food supplier is less than its current year consumption time. Then, the food supplier can attempt to find whether what factors to cause the past food consumers do not choose to increase food purchase times to the food supplier in current year. The factors may bc possible be the food supplier's food prices are raised, food quality or taste is poor, the different kinds of food supply is shortage challenge, the food supplier's consumers lose confidence to buy the food supplier's foods to eat, when (AI) big data gather tool can help the food suppliers to find what the main factors to cause the past food consumer number to be reduced in order to predict how future food consumers' behavioral changes will be influenced from the food supplier's competitors in the global food supply market. Hence, (AI) big data gather tool can help every food supplier to attempt to find what the main factors to case the food supplier's food consumer number to be reduced as well as it can help the food supplier to predict how the food supplier's potential (past not every purchase its any food consumers) food consumers who can be persuaded to choose to buy its foods to eat by learning what the main factors influence.

In conclusion, (AI) big data gather tool can help the food supplier to find what the main factors influence its past food consumers do not choose to buy its food more times or find what the main factors will attract its potential (not ever buying its foods consumes) food consumers to choose to buy the food supplier's foods to eat.

6.2 The challenges of (AI) big data gather shaping
the future of retail for consumer industries

Another challenge of (AI) big data gather is that how to shape the consumer behavior to let business owner to feel or know oe predict. It means that how it express it's conclusion or opinion for every consumer behavior after it had gather all big data in any data gather period, e.g. three months, half year or one year consumer shopping model data gather period.

Because every kind of industry, consumers will continue to demand price and quality change , with a wide range of convenient fulfilment options among of different kinds of products or services supply. Overall, the (AI) big data gather procedure gives opinion concerns every time retail experience will become more exciting, simple and convenient, depending on the consumer's ever-changing needs. So, I believe that (AI) big data gather every conclusion or result will be different, due to consumer's price and quality demand will often change to every kind of product or service supply in retail industry. So, how to shape (AI) big data gathering's analytical conclusion or result more clear. I shall recommend organizations need to build great understanding of and a stronger connection to increasingly empowered consumers before they plan and implement how to apply (AI) big data gather tool to predict consumer behavior as below:

Firstly, (AI) is empowered by technology, the consumer is redefining value. The traditional measures of cost, choice and convenience are still relevant, but not control and experience are also important. Globally, consumers have access to more than 2 billion different products choice by a wide range of traditional competitors and dynamic new entrants, all experimenting with new business models and methods of client engagement.

As choice increases, loyalty becomes more difficult familiarity and the consumer becomes more empowered. Businesses will have no choice and constantly innovate and disrupt themselves by meeting new technologies of high standards and expectations of consumers. So, (AI) data gather tool will need to follow different target group of consumers' needs to follow their different kinds of product design or style choice preferable to gather data in order to conclude the different target groups of consumer behavior to give opinion more clear and accurate to let businessmen to understand more clear how its customers' behavioral choice trend in the future half month, even to two years period.

Secondly, businessmen need to adopt changing technologies rapidly. Technology will be the key driver of this retail industry. Industry participants will only success if they have a clear prediction to focus on how to using technology to increase the value added to consumers. They must , however, do so will I realistic assessment of their costs and benefits. Hence, (AI) big data gather technological tools will need to design to help them to gather data efficiently by these ways, such as the internet of things (IOT), artificial intelligence (AI) machine learning, augmented reality (AR)/virtual reality (VR), digital traceability. So, future (AI) big data gather tool are predicted to be most influential customer behavioral positive emotion changing tool for retail , due to their widespread applications , ability to drive efficiencies and impact on labor in order to impact consumer behavior changing effort from negative emotion to positive.

Thirdly, (AI) big data gather tool is an advanced data science of consumer behavior predictive tool. Businesses will have to bring the journey from simply collecting consumer data to using it to scale and systematize enhanced decision making across the entire value chain. When focused on their business goals, industry players should not lose sight of the impact that future capabilities and transformative business models may have on society.

However, (AI) big data gather tool will encounter these challenges when any business plans and implements to apply it to predict consumer behavior in retail industry. The challenges include that as below:

1. The high cost and difficulty of implementing new technologies . The (AI) big data gather tool needs capital and capabilities to be designed to implement to be applied to different retail industry users. so, expensive barriers to innovation, an organization and the skillsets of its people to support a new design of (AI) big data gather tool, highly digital technology may be required.

2. Slow pace of cultural change. Consumers need to adapt or accept (AI) new technology consumption model in the traditional retail industry. The rate of change is outpacing the ability of businesses to keep up. (AI) big data gather tool needs to be designed to adopt in new or evolved business model requires, in most cases, a new level of customer behavioral predictive machine operation will impact to influence any retail businesses' consumer behavioral changes at a minimum, an organization's structure, capabilities, culture and decision making. If the retail business expects to apply (AI) big data gather tool to predict how to change its consumer behaviors and how their consumption behaviors will tend to change in order to achieve to change their positive emotion from negative emotion before they choose to buy its product or consume its service in success.

6.3 Challenge to using (AI) neural networks to predict customer behavior from big data gather tool

(AI) big data gather tool will encounter the challenge: How can predict customer behavior be represented as sequential data describing the interactions of the customer with a company or an (AI) data gather system through the time, e.g. these interactions are items that the customer purchase or views ? So, every customer data gather , (AI) needs to spend time to analyze how and why to cause whose consumption behavioral choice. It is too difficult matter or judgement for (AI) learning. So, (AI) needs to spend time to learn how to analyze every customer's shopping behavior or actin in order to gather all different consumers' past shopping action information in order to help business owners to predict future its potential customer shopping behavior how to change more clear and accurate prediction.

(AI) big data gather tool needs to learn to know that how to judge every customer interaction likes purchases over time can be represented with sequential data. Sequential data has the main property that the order of the information is important. Many (AI) machine learning models are not suited for sequential data, as they consider each input sample independent from previous ones. Therefore, at the end of the sequence, (AI) big data gather learn machines need to keep in their internal state of every customer purchase data, kind of product or service, price , whole year consumption times form all previous inputs, making them suitable for this type of data.

However, consumer behavior can be represented as sequential data describing the interactions through the time. Examples of these interactions are the items that the user purchases or views. Therefore, the history of interactions can be modeled as sequential data, which has the particular trial that an incorporate a temporal aspect. For example, if a user buys a new mobile phone, who might purchase accessories for this mobile phone in the near future or it the user buys a electronic book or paper book , he might be interested in books by the same author. Therefore, to make accurate predictions is important to model this temporal aspect correctly. To solve this predictive challenge of consumers to buy the product. One count the number of purchased products of a particular category in the last N days, or the number of days since the last purchase.

So, the (AI) big data gather designers can attempt to produce a feature vector which can be fed into a machine learning algorithm such as " logistic regression" will be the main feature and function to any (AI) big data gather machine to learn how to apply this " logistic regression" function or feature to predict any customer behavioral change for any product purchase or service consumption to the (AI) predictive consumer behavioral business users. Every different kinds of product purchases or services consumption will be needed to design " different model of logistic regression" in order to follow the kind of business to predict whose consumer purchase or service consumption behavior to predict more accurate.

6.4 Challenges of artificial intelligence, algorithms technology and machine learning impact to consumption market

Markets have played a key role in providing individuals and businesses with the opportunity to gain from trade. If (AI) big data gather tool can predict how to change potential customer behavior in success. The challenges to consumers will face that the overall market consumption model will be dominated by the businessmen only. So, it is not fair or reasonable to consumers, because (AI) big data gather tool has controlled or dominated all consumers' minds and it has predicted how and why every kind of product or service consumer shopping model or consumption behaviors how will change.

It will bring this questions: How can market designers learn the characteristics necessary to set optimal, or at least better, reserve prices after they had gather all data to conclude the analytical results of their consumers behaviors how will change? How can market designers better learn the environments of their markets?

In response to these challenges, artificial intelligence (AI) and machine learning are important tools for market design. For example, retailers and marketplaces , such as eBay, Amazon and many others are mining their vast amounts of data to identity patterns that help them create better shopping experiences for their clients and increase the efficiency of their markets. By having better prediction tools, these and their companies can predict and better manage dynamic consumption market environments. The improved forecasting that (AI) and machine learning algorithms provide help marketplaces and retailers better anticipate consumer demand and producer supply as well as help target products and activities for segmented markets. Another important application of (AI) 's strength in improving forecasting to help markets operate more efficiently is in electricity market example. To operate efficiently, electricity marker makers can attempt to apply (AI) machine learning tool to follow every household family electricity consumers' past electricity consumption record to judge (predict) how it will be every family's forecasting in the year.

An inaccurate forecast in the electricity supply and demand that can dramatically affect electricity market bad supply outcomes causing high variance in electricity charge prices or worse, blackouts. By better predicting every family's electricity demand and supply , electricity market makers can better allocate power generation to the most efficient power sources and maintain a more reasonable electricity stable charge market. Any example is design market, the application of (AI) algorithms to market design are already widespread and diverse.

(AI) algorithms technology , it is a safe that (AI) will play a growing role in the design and implementation of market over a wide range of applications. The challenges are that how (AI) can guarantee accurate to predict when and why and how consumer behavioral changes to any retail industries. In fact, retailers will need to discover the value that (AI) can bring to what benefits to influence their customer behaviors.

In the future, (AI) will bring their benefits to influence customers to build positive emotions to any retailers in these aspects as below:

1. Future (AI) big data gather tool will be an area of compute science that deals with giving machines , the ability to seem like they have human intelligence. In short, it is the power of a machine to copy intelligent human behavior. For examaple, machine learning algorithms are being integrated into analytics and customer relationship management platforms to uncover information on how to better serve customers, chat bots have been incorporated into websites to provide immediate service to customers.

2. (AI) adoption continue to rise with chat bots taking the lead. Due to increasing ease of deployment , instant availability and improved quality, chat bots will become more and more common to manage customer service queries and to make intelligent purchase recommendations. Also, retailers can engage this kind of technology to answer continue questions and supplement customer support with chat-based shopping experience. So, (AI) and declines personalized, customized and localized experiences to customers.

(AI) will be applied across the entire retail product and service cycle, firm manufacturing to post-sale customer service interactions. Hence, retailers can use (AI) to its fullest potential will be also to influence purchases in the moment and anticipate future purchases, guiding shoppers towards the right products in a regular and highly personalized manner.

3. (AI) technology can rise the conscious customers. Customers are demanding an increased interest in the ethical practice of the brands they buy from. Todays, customers have a well-developed sense of what is solely intended to drive sales. This has lead to a rise in consumers ho make values based judgements about what to buy and where to shop. These

consumers believe their purchase habits have an impact on the world. To win customers, retailers need have good conscious to predict consumers' desire. Future, (AI) data gather technology will be a good consumer behavior predictive tool to predict about for years will now become customer expectations and will have drastically changed the path to purchase. So, (AI) data gather tool is the predictive consumer expectations tool on every interaction, they have these brands.

4. Future (AI) can be impacted to influence consumer behaviors by its potential to free up time, enhance, quality, and enhance personalization. The industries include: Healthcare industry can apply (AI) to support diagnosis by detecting variations in patient data, early identification of potential pandemics, imaging diagnostics; automat industry can apply (AI) to autonomous fleets to ride sharing, semi-autonomous features, such as driver assist, engine monitoring and predictive, autonomous maintenance; financial service industry can apply (AI) to design the suitable personalized financial planning, fraud detection and anti-money laundering and automation of customer operation; transportation and logistics industry can apply (AI) to autonomous trucking and delivery, traffic control and reduced congestion and enhanced security; technology, media and telecommunications industry can apply (AI) to search media, and recommendation, customized content creation and personalized marketing and advertising to attract retailers to promote; retail and consumer industry can apply (AI) to design personalized production, anticipating customer demand, , inventory and delivery management; energy industry can apply (AI) to read and record smart metering , more efficient grid operation and storage and predictive maintenance; manufacturing industry can apply (AI) to enhance monitoring and auto-correction of processes, supply chain and production optimization and on-demand production.

Hence, future (AI) technology will impact consumer technology when any retailers apply it to assist its manufacturing processes or product sale or service provision processes to satisfy consumers‘ needs, it means that it can help any retailers to influence positive emotion to consumers in their whole sale or consumption or purchase proccesses.

5. (AI) and machine learning technologies make it possible to capture, process, and inter data on a massive scale effectively , then any human being could ever do. For example, Criteo's creative technology " Kinetic design" can apply insights from 1.2 billion monthly impressions to select and optimize individual branded advertisements components according to

each shopper's preference and intent. This ensures more personalization and visually inspiring on brand ads. resulting in up to 12% more sales for (AI) technology advertiser clients.

Moreover, advertisers can now engage and inspire shoppers on a more personal level, rendering custom ads. it real-time for every impression. So, designer continues to learn from each design's success to make ads. more and more effective over time. Furthermore, brands are increasingly using paid search on retail sites to draw attention to their products on the crowded online shelf, e.g. Google shopping is a key growth area's more users are engaging with shopping ads. and across the globe. Google shopping has become essential to retailers' marketing strategies, but is a difficult channel to apply its tool to be promoted effectively . Thus, future (AI) and machine -learning technologies can dramatically improve digital commerce performance application to apply (AI) and machine learning to digital consumer. So, future (AI) technology can be applied to digital commerce aspect, it will fall into the categories of pattern recognition, classification, prediction and consumer behavior.

In conclusion, the benefits of using (AI) in digital commerce include: improved efficiency in discovering the relationships between datasets over traditional methods, which require complex modeling and coding, improved accuracy for clearly defined processes that involve a lot of manual processing, ability to deal with a large emotion of data with many attributes, for example: customer behavior data, multichannel and multi-device data , complex product data and fraud detection, more accurate analysis, such as customer segmentation sentiment, analysis and personalization frequent algorithum refreshes, such as several times a day, to capture the changes in customer and market behavior.

Finally, however, a lot of types predictive consumption behavior around (AI), in particulars that driven by vendors claiming their solutions are (AI) , ready and can deliver dramatic improvements over existing technologies. Application leaders for digital commerce can be misled into believing that (AI) can solve all their problems, which is not true for n in-depth discussion of the (AI) consumers and market behavioral predictive tool and machine -learning technologies bot. Thus, (AI) prediction consumer behavioral technology can give beneficial quantitative analysis for forecasting in business and market especially in consumer behavior and in the consumer decision-making process (consumer choice model) more effectively and efficiently.

Chapter seven

Is Artificial Intelligent the most effective and accurate consumer behavioral tool?

Is (AI) the best and the most effective and accurate consumer behavioral prediction tool to compare other kinds of consumer behavioral prediction tools? Nowadays, retailing competitions are serious businessmen often find different kinds of methods to attempt to predict consumer changes. The consumer behavioral predictive methods can include as these below methods, instead of (AI) big data gathering tool.

Firstly, statistics is the popular mathematic method, it applies auto-regression, liner regression, structural equation modelling, logistic regression statistic techniques to be used to predict consumer behaviors. Secondly, it is classification method, it sis a support vector machine to assist businessmen to make consumer behavioral prediction, it also includes decision making tress diagram technique. Thirdly, it is rule mining method, it is algorithm, market base analytic etc. business marketing concept analytical tool, it also includes graph mining technique tool. Next, it is psychological prediction model tool, it is psychology prediction model too, it is a kind of psychological method to predict consumer behaviors. Finally, it is the most updated and potential artificial neural network (ANN) machine tool, it gathered big data, then it will carry on analyzing and applies psychological method to conclude the most accurate and reasonable solutions to give recommendation to businesses to predict when and how and why their consumer behaviors will change. So, it is one owned human mind's machine and owned psychological and analytical efforts to replace humans to make any judgement in order to make the most accurate predictive behavioral changes for consumers, instead of the traditional marketing concept and psychological and mathematic methods to predict consumer behavior, (AI) big data gathering tool will be another new tool.

What are the advantages of (AI) tool to be used to predict consumer behaviors as well as what are the different between it and other traditional consumer behavioral predictive tools? I shall explain as below:

Firstly, as above all case studies are explained to (AI) questionnaire design method benefit, I believe (AI) big data gathering tool can be applied to help human to analyze and design any the suitable valid questions to enquire any kinds of business consumers in order to gather the most meaning and useful opinions to conclude the most accurate consumer behavioral prediction for every questionnaire. So, future (AI)'s analytical effort and decision making effort most be exceed above human's judgement efforts. So, future (AI) can help human to design the most useful and meaning different kinds of valid questionnaire (survey) questions as well as assist humans to analyze and make accurate decision making and conclusions to give opinions to help businessmen to predict when consumer behaviors will change and how their consumption behaviors will change to influence their businesses in order to help them to make any efficient and effective and accurate solutions to avoid consumer number to be decreased and the most important benefit is that it can give opinions to help businessmen to explain why (what the factors) cause their consumer behaviors change suddenly. It will be human's efforts can not achieve to exceed (AI)'s efforts in the future.

Secondly, (AI) can make artificial machine judgement and analytical effort, without human misleading or unfair or unreasonable judgement. So, it can make more fair and reasonable and accurate conclusion to give opinions to predict when, how and why consumer behaviors will change suddenly to the kind of business in customer model building process and evaluating the results of customer relationship management –related investment more accurate.

Furthermore, (AI) big data gathering tool will help businesses to improve the success rate of acquiring customers, increasing sales and establishing competitiveness. (AI) big data gathering tool can give opinions how to build customer loyalty to be positive emotion impact and it can find solutions to avoid every client's negative emotion causes to bring complaints behavior to the businessman's product or service. For example, Telecom industry and aggressive research has been conducted in this by applying various data mining techniques to avoid long distance phone call users' complaints. If gathered any long distance phone call users' past complaint data to record what are their general complaint issues. Then, (AI) tool will analyze all these past complaint issues to conclude and give opinions to let Telecom knows whether which aspects encounter challenge that Telecom needs to improve it's long distance phone call services or functions in order to satisfy Telecom's long distance phone call users' needs for long term. After Telecom attempted to improve its services and/ or functions from (AI) opinions and solution methods, when it fell it's long distance phone call users have positive emotions to satisfy its service performance and function performance. Then, it can prove (AI) tool's opinions and solutions are useful. The consequence is that their complain numbers will be decreased and they won't plan to choose another long distance phone call telephone service company to replace Telecom long distance phone call service more easily.

So, (AI) big data gathering tool can concentrate on finding focus on components of customer relationship management method and datasets more accurate and efficient and effective than human's data gathering and analytical effort. It implies (AI) big data gathering tool has unique more efficient and effective and accurate dataset gathering and analytical and judgement and decision making effort, it is human can not achieve.

Thirdly, (AI) big data gathering tool has much customer loyalty predictive effort. It's effort is more easily subsequently selected, reviewed and classified to compare human's gathering data effort in whole data gathering and analytical process.

In (AI) big data gathering process, (AI) can organize whole big data gathering process and technique more easily in short time. It will include these four steps. The first stage is that customer identification stage, customer identification also known as acquisition has to do with targeting the population , who are most likely to become customer segmentation. So, (AI) can help different kinds of businesses to gather their competitors' consumer purchase behavior data in short time, it is human can not achieve. The second stage is that customer attraction stage, after (AI) maker has been segmented for the business when it has ensured to gather the businessman's global competitors' consumers data. Then it analyze these all data to find solutions / methods to give the best opinions to the organizations how to achieve the direct effort and resources into attracting the target customer segments. The third stage is that customer retention, it can be defined as the activity that an organization undertakes in order to reduce customer defections. TO be successful, customer retention starts with the first contact on organization has with a customer and continues throughout the entire lifetime of a relationship involves loyalty programs, one to one marketing and complaints management. SO, (AI) can consist the business to find the best or the most reasonable , efficient , effective solutions or methods and it will conclude all these solutions to find the most reasonable and useful opinions to achieve to the aim to help the business to reduce customer complain numbers and help the business to build confident loyalty relationship between it and its clients. SO, (AI)'s analytical effort and decision making effort can be more accurate than human's analytical effort and decision making effort. IT can achieve it's consumer behavioral predictive aim more accurate and efficient and effective in the shortest time to compare human.

Fourthly, (AI) big data gathering tool can design more accurate dataset program for questionnaire (survey) to compare human's questionnaire (survey) effort. It means that (AI) can spend less time to research and make judgement what are the most reasonable and meaning questions for different kinds of businesses' needs. This includes data conduction a questionnaire, survey or interview of the individual or environment researched, public data repository: This includes commercially available public data; organizational data; this contains data collected from an organizational database, organizational information system. For example, their website log details etc. It also includes company transactional data, data purchased from a company.

For example, one vehicle sale company expects to research all global vehicle sale companies' past the different kinds of vehicle styles, design sale number data, the different kinds of vehicle style, design sale price data, every country's vehicle consumer number to the vehicle purchase number data to the vehicle company in short time. (AI) big data gathering tool can help the vehicle sale company to gather all any one for these global vehicle sale competitors' past data in the short time. It is human effort, who can not achieve this efficient, effective and accurate data gathering aim for this vehicle sale company. Even, when (AI) had gathered all global it's vehicle competitors' past sale data, (AI) can make more accurate analytical and judgement and decision making effort to design different kinds of questionnaire (survey) questions to prepare to enquire it's different target segmentation vehicle potential clients in order to predict what are their needs to choose to buy any vehicles from the vehicle company. SO, (AI) tool can conclude more accurate conclusions and give the most reasonable and useful opinions to let the vehicle company to know in order to predict what are it's potential vehicle buyer's needs and manufacture the suitable vehicle styles or designs to raise their vehicle purchase desires.

Fifthly, (AI) tool is only one perfect tool for big data gathering in order to achieve accurate results and increased profit. What is (AI) big data gathering mean? The term " big data"gathering describes the accumulation and analytical of vast amounts of information, but big data is much more than a big amount of data. It is also the ability to extract meaning to sort through big volumes of numbers and find the hidden patterns, unexpected correlations and surprising connections that can be used in different industries like medical field, security and protection field or marketing that adopt " big data driven" decision making enjoy significantly greater productivity than those that do not. So, the benefits of (AI) is given to the company by using big data repaid complexity of implementation projects and hence project risks, when accelerating time to valuc. It is why that human's gathering effort can not replace (A I) data gathering effort.

All analysing above benefits to (AI) big data benefits to any organizations, it brinfs this question: How can (AI)apply big data gathering and analyzing to predict when and how any why consumer behavior will change suddenly? The purchase decision making process is consumers reducing purchase choice behaviors.

Consumers are being considered pure rational beings (consumer tried only to satisfy self-interest). Hence, due to future (AI) owns human's psychological , analytical , emotional predictive, purchasing decision making effort.

(A I) will be assumed to sees one customer how who will make purchase decisions. So, after the (AI) gathered all data concerns the find of business's past customer segmentation purchase activities, e.g. age, sex,. Income level, the product's style sale number, the product price variable sale etc. different kinds complex data.

It can makemore accurate psychological and analytical effort to predict when the business's consumer behaviors will change as behaviors will change as well as find what reasons their consumption behaviors will change and how trend of their consumer behaviors will change more accurate. For example, today there are a lot of industries that use big data: healthcare (treatment) becoming personalized and patient centric and predictive analysis are used to prevent diseases for example Angelina Jolie underevent a predictive double mastectomy after learning she had 87% rich to developing breast cancer, sports (by using sensors data are collected from players during a game in order to improve their playing schemes), weather(more than 60 years of global weather analysis are used to predict the risk of future extreme events), logistics (smart tucks and smart species, agriculture (monitoring weather and soil conditions for optimum point of harvesting).

Consequently, due to the evolving consumer demands, and the ever growing digitization, the world is digitally transforming which means the new technologies are needed to be used and driven significant business improvement. So, such as why (AI) tool will be our future main predictive tool to help businesses to predict when, how and why their potential customer behavioral will change. Big data is one of the our channels through digital transformation is made, together with cloud, mobile and networks. The challenges for digital transforming and therefore using A I big data gathering tool as main technology are: digital proficiency, legacy systems, security and jobs becoming absolute.

In the future, big data can use data from text to picture , sounds, movies, musics satellite coordinates or any other type of input or output data that type of input or uouput data that came from different influential aspect. It is cloud solutions, bring big data will be for predict insight driven by business stategy, new product strategies and new consumer relationship, predictive consumer behavioral strategy. Using the right data in the right business decision will mean smart decisions, new opportunitites and utimately a big competitive advantage.Hence (AI) big data gathering tool is different is that (AI) can be one depth in-memeory database function, it can make real-time data analytics that provide meaningful information in short time, it is also the visualization tool , such as SAP Lumira, allow this exploration and understanding of the data, and ultimately supports the decision making process. All above these features, which will be human's data gathering effort who won't exceed (AI) big data gathering effort. Hence, future (AI)big data gathering will be the best choice to assist businesses to predict consumer behaviors successfully.

Reference

Adrian, P. (2012). Introduction to marketing theory & practice, 3 rd edition, London: Oxford press.

Ajzen, I (1991). The theory of planned behavior. Organizational behavior and human decision processes, 50(2), 179-211. doi: 10.1016/0749.5978 (91) 90020-7.

Alba, Joseph W. and J. Wesley Hutchinson (1987). " Dimensions Of Consumer Expertise", Journal of consumer research, 13 March, 411-454.

Bailey, L., Mokhtarian, P.L. Little, A. (2008). The broader Connection Between Public Transportation, Energy Conservation And Greenhouse Gas Reduction, Report Prepared As Part Of TCRP Project J-11/Tasks Transit Cooperative Research Program, Transportation Research Board Submitted To American Public Transportation Association in http://www.apta.com/research/into/online/land_use.cfmi, accessed 17 April 2008.

Baucer, R,"Consumer Bhavior As Risk Taking , In Risk Taking And Information handling In Consumer Behavior", D. Coxceds Harvard University Press, Cambridge, Mass 1976.

Biederman, P. (2008). Travel and tourism, Pearson Prentice Hall, New Jersey.

Bogers, R. P., Brug, J. Van Assema, P., & Dagnetie, P.C. (2004) , Explaining fruit and vegetable consumption: The theory of planned behavior and misconception of personal intake level. Appetite, 42,157-166.

Bolton, Ruth N. (1998), " A Dynamic Model Of The Duration Of The Customer's Relationship With A Continuous Service Provider: The Role Of Satisfaction", Marketing Science, 17 (1), 45-65.

B.Shiv and A. Fedorikhin, " Heart And Min In Conflict: The Interplay Of affect And Cognition In Consumer Decision Making", J. Consumer Res., vol. 26, pp. 278-292, Dec. 1999.

Brown, K.W., Ryan, R.M. Reswell , J.D. (2007). Mindfulness: Theoretical Foundatins And Evidence For Its Salutary Effects. Psychological Inquiry, 18, 211-237.

Burke, R.R. : Behavioral effects of digital signage, J. Advertising Res. 49(2), 180-185 (2009).

Cant, M., Brink , A. & Brijall, S., Consumer behavior, Cape Town, South Africa: Juta, 2006.

Conner, M. & Abraham, C. (2001). Conscientiousness and the theory of planned behavior: Toward a more complete model of the antecedents of intention and behavior. Social psychology bulletin, 27, 1547-1561.

Cooper C. Mallon, K, Leadbetter S, Pollack L, Peipins (2005) , cancer internet search activity on a major search engine, United States 2001 to 2003, J Med Internet Res. 7(3): e36.

Cope, R. R. Cope and H. Davis (2008). Disney's virtual Queues: A strategic opportunity to co-brand services ? Journal of Business & economics research, vol. 6 no10, 13-20.

Cornelia, B.F. (1999) Rural development news, the North Central Regional Center For Rural Development vol. no 24 , IOWA.

Couper, M.P. J. Blair and T. Triplet (1999). A Comparison Of Mail And E-mail For a Survey Of Employees In USA Statistical Agencies. Journal Of Official Statistics, 15, 39-56.

David J. Nowak & Gordon M. Melsler (2016) " Air quality effects of urban trees and parks." National recreation and park association, USA.

Data monitor (2008). The proctor and gamble company. Retrieved Nov. 15 2009 from http://www.datamonitor.com/

De Hollander, A. E. M., J.M. Melse, Elebret & P. G.N. Kramers (1999), " An Aggregate public health indicator to represent the impact of multiple environmental exposures" Epidemiology: 606-617.

De Visser, R.O., & McDonnell, E.J. (2013). " Man points": Masculine capital and young men's health. Health psychology, 32(1), 5-14. doi:10. 1037/a0029045.

Dunn, J & A Neumsister (2002). Knowledge management in the Information age. E. business review, Fall , 37-45. Jounral of service, spring 2011, vol. 4, no1, De Grovte (2009).

Dyer, D., F. Dalzell & R. Olegario (2004). Rising tide. Lessons learned from 165 years of brand building at Procter and Gamble. Boston, MA: Havard Business School Press.

Eysenbach G (2006) Infodemiology: Tracking flu- related searches on the web for syndromic surveillance. American Medical Informatics Associaion Annual Symposium Proceedings , Curran Associates, Red Hook, NY, pp. 244-248.

Ettredge M, Gerdes, J. Karuga , G (2005) Using web- based search data to predict macro-economic statistics. Commun ACM 48: 87-92.

Felce, D. and Perry, J. (1995). Quality of life: A contribution to its definition and measurement, vol. 16, no.1 pp: 51-74.

Feldman, Jack M. And John G. Lynch Jr. (1988), "Self-
Generated Validity And Other Effects Of Measurement On Belife, Attitude, Intention And Behavior", Journal of applied psychology, 73(3),421-35.

Fiese, M, Hofmann, W., & Wanke, M (2009). The impulsive consumer. Predicting consumer behavior with implicit reaction time measurement. In M. Wanke (ed.) Social psychology of consumer behavior (pp.335-364). New York, NY: Psychology press.

Fitzsimons, Gavan, J. And Vicki G. Morwitz (1996), " The Effect Of Measuring Intent On Brand-Level
Purchase Behavior", Journal of consumer research, 23 (1), 1-11.

Hallerman , D. (2008) video Advertising Online: Spending And Pricing , New York. E-Marketer.

Harriet Griffey. (2010) The art of concentration, enhance focus, Reduce, stress and achieve move. Macmillan publishers ltd,Basinastoke and Oxford, London UK.

Helleman, D. (2008) Video Advertising Online: Spending And Pricing , New York, E-Marketer.

Hensen, C. (2003). Kreuzfahrtourismus.www.christoph- hensen.de/ Facharbeit.pdf.

Huang, H.I. (2012). An empirical analysis of the strategic Management of competitive advantage: a case study of higher technical and vocational education in Taiwan (Doctoral dissertation,
Victoria University).

Jamieson, Linda F. And Frank M. Bass (1989), " Adjusting Stated Intention Measures To Predict Trial Purchase Of New Products: A Comparison Of Models And Methods," Journal of marketing research, 26 (August), 336-45.

Korea Ministry Of Environment. Public Organizations spend 2.2 Trillon Korean Won To Purchase green Products in 2014; Ministry Of Environment: Sejoung, Korea, 2015.

Kremers, S.P. J., De Bruijn, G.J., droomers, M., Van Lenthe, F. J., & Brug, J. (2005). Environmental interventions for selected dietary behaviors in adults. In J. Brug & F. J. Van Lenthe (eds.) , Environmental determinants and interventions for physical activity, nutrition and smoking: A review pp. 282-315. Rotterdam: Erasmus Medical Center.

Lee, D.; Kim, M. ; Lee, J. adoption of green electricity policies: Investigating the role of environmental attitudes via big data-driven search-queries. Energy policy 2016. 90, 187-201.

Lee, Terrence, " Tech in Asia-connecting Asia's startup system " Tech. in Asia- connecting Asia's startup ecosystem, N.p.,4 July 2016.

Los Angeles Country Department Of public Health (2016), Country Health Ranking Model, Retrieved From www.countryhealthrankgings.org/our-approach. USA.

Mayne, Lonnie. " Evolve of die in the age of the consumer". Entrepreneur, N.P. , 16 Apr. 2014. web of Oct. 2016.

McGregor, S.L. T., & Goldsmith, E.B. (1998). Expanding our understanding of quality of life, standard of living and well-being. Journal of family and consumer science, 90(2), 2-6, 22.

McMichael, A.J. M. Mckee, J. Shkolnikov and T. Valkanen (2004), " Morality trends and setbacks, global convergence or divergence?", Lancet 363, 1155-1159.

Melse, J.M. & A.E. M. De Hollander (2001). " Human Health And The Environment", background document for the OECD Environmental Outlook, OECD, Paris.

Moschis, George p. & Roy, L. Moore (1979), " Decision making among the young. A socialization perspective " Journal of consumer research , 6 (September).

Mulligan, M. Banerjee, T & Thomas, N. (2008) ,European Paid Content And Activity Forecast, (2008 to 2013), Jupiter Research.

Peter, J., Ryan, M, M, " An Investigation Of Perceived Risk At The Brand Level, " Journal of marketing research, 13 May 1976, pp. 184-188.

Pieters, R., & Wedel, M. (2007). Goal Control Of Visual Attention To Advertising: The Yarbus Implication. Journal Of Consumer Research, 34, 224-233 (August).

Parasuaman, and Leonard L. Berry (1985), " Problems And Strategies In Sevices Marketing", Journal of marketing, 49 (Spring), 33-46.

Priesnitz, W. (2007) Counting Our Food Miles. Natural Life, 1 July.

R.C. Oliver, " When is consumer loyalty?" J.Marketing vol. 63, pp.33-44.1999.

Reggiani, A . (ed). 1998, accessibility, trade and locational behavior, Ashgate publishing ltd, England.

Rushe, D. (2013) " The 10 best paid CEO in America". The Guardian , 22 Oct, (online). Available at: http://www.theguardian.com/business/2013/Oct22/best-paid-chief-executives-america (Accessed: 3 May 2014).

Spiekermann and Wegener (2007), update of selected potential accessibility indicators. Final report, urban and regional research (S&W), RRG spatial planning and geoinformation. ESPON. Available online at http:// <www.espon.eu/mmp/online/website/ contentprojects/947/ 1297/file_2724/espon_accessibility_update-2006-fr_070207.pdf>, accessed on 1 July 2009.

Starbucks (2014) Our company available at http:// www. starbucks.com/about- us/company-information (accessed: 3 May 2014).

Shostack, G. Lynn (1984), " Designing Services That Deliver", Harvard Business Review, 62 (January-February), 133-9.

Shostack, G. Lynn (1985), " Planning The Service Encounter ,in the service encounter" , John A. Czepiel, Michael R. Solomon, and Carol F. Suprenant, eds. New York: Lexington Books, 243-54.

Shostack, G. Lynn (1987), " Service Positioning Through, Structural Change", Journal of marketing, 51 (Janurary), 34-43.

Soloman, Michael R. (1985), "Packaging The Service Provider", Service Industries Journal , 5(1), 64-71.

Stevens, C.W. (1980), "K-MartStores Try New Look To Invite More Spending" The Wall Street Journal, Nov. 26, 29-35.

Sullivan, Nicholas P(2007). You can hear me now: How Micro loans and cell phones are connecting the world, San Francisco, CA: John Wilsey & Sans, 2007.

T. Ambler, A. Ioannides, And S. Rose, " Brand s On The Brain : Neuroimages Of Advertising ", Business Strategy rev., vol. 11, 3. pp. 17-30. 2000.

Westbrook, Robert A. (1980), " Intrapersonal affective influences on consumer satisfaction with products, " Journal of consumer research , 7 (June) 49-54.

Wiig, k.(1993). Knowledge management foundations: Thinking About thinking. How people and organizations create, represent and use knowledge vol.1 , of knowledge management series schema press: Arlington, TX.

World Health Organization (2003). Diet, nutrition and the prevention of Chronic diseases report of a joint WHO/FAO. expert consultation. Geneva: World Health Organization.

Wysocki, B. (1979), " Sight, Smell, Sound: They're all arms in retailer's arsenal" The Wall Street Journal, Nov. 17, 1979. 1-35.

Yale Center For Environmental Law And Policy (2006). Environmental Performance Index. Data available on-line at http://epi.yale.edu

www.ingramcontent.com/pod-product-compliance
Ingram Content Group UK Ltd.
Pitfield, Milton Keynes, MK11 3LW, UK
UKHW040604210726
13854UKWH00009B/2618